To Billy;
Thanks
It is a very nice bit of work.
Ken

Last Roll Call

By Kenneth S. Tucker

Kenneth S. Tucker 11-07-09

and Wanda Tucker Goodwin

Priority Publishing Company

Last Roll Call

by Kenneth S. Tucker and
Wanda Tucker Goodwin

Priority Publishing Company
6804 Sandra Road
Southport, FL 32409
850-819-5998
www.priority-publishing.com

ISBN 978-0-9754749-5-2

About the Cover

Standing L to R: S/Sgt. Kenneth Tucker - tail gunner, 2nd Lt. Halsey Nisula - navigator, 1st Lt. Louis Dunigan - pilot, substitute co-pilot. Kneeling L to R: S/Sgt. Jack Taylor - ball-turret gunner, Flight Officer Donald McQuistion - bombardier, T/Sgt. Clyde Dwight - flight engineer, S/Sgt. Michael Joyce - right-waist gunner.

This picture was taken by Doc Remley our flight surgeon. We had just returned from a very rough mission and the two guys who were flying fill-in that day for our radio operator and left-waist gunner didn't stick around. We had a regular radio operator on the crew but we had kicked him out. Before we left the states we had been ordered to leave our left-waist gunner behind. Our regular copilot, 2nd Lt. James Garrison, was sick that day. I don't recall the mission, but it was before we were shot down. We went down in the *Kwiturbitchin* on Christmas Day of 1944.

This book is dedicated to the bomber crew members of World War II who made the supreme sacrifice - they are the real heroes.

Kenneth S. Tucker

M/Sgt. USAF Retired

Preface

Kenneth S. Tucker

The idea of writing my memoir was planted when I was still in high school. During my senior year, my English teacher, Shirley Rehberg, knew that I would be going in service soon so she asked me to keep a diary. She promised that, when I returned, she would help me write my memoir. She convinced me that the journey I was about to make was worthy of being recorded for future generations.

In 1984, while visiting friends in Ipswich, England, we made a stop at the local RAF Club. One of the RAF officers joined our party and seemed thrilled to learn that I had been on a bomber crew during the war. He had nothing but praise for the American bomber boys and wanted to know all about my experiences. He told me that I would be doing my family an injustice if I did not pass my experiences on to future generations.

Over the years, I never forgot about writing my memoir; it just seemed that I was always distracted by so many other projects. So, when my oldest daughter, Wanda, retired and offered to help me with the venture, I eagerly accepted.

I always felt that I did have a story to tell. One of my first objectives was to emphasize the role of the 15th Air Force in ending the war. In doing so, I did not want to take away any of the glory given to the 8th Air Force out of England because they certainly deserved all the credit they received. I did, however, want to inform readers that the 15th Air Force out of Italy played a huge role in ending the war in Europe by concentrating bombing runs on the German's petroleum supply. I have always believed that the accomplishments of the 15th were overshadowed by the huge amount of publicity given the 8th by the war correspondents and touring dignitaries who would never have set foot in the pitiful environment that we lived in.

My story isn't just about me; it's about my crew.

Without them, I wouldn't have a story to tell. By getting to know the members of just one bomber crew, I can only hope that readers will come to understand and appreciate the sacrifices that so many thousands of young men made for our country.

When this book is published, my daughter and I plan to attempt to locate the children of some of my crew. I would especially like to find the families of our pilot, Louis Dunigan and our flight engineer, Clyde Dwight. These two characters certainly provided me with lots of quality material for "Last Roll Call." What a thrill it would be for me to personally present their children a copy of the book in honor of their fathers.

Acknowledgements

Putting the memories of my experiences of the World War II years down on paper has been far more difficult than I had anticipated. In the past, I had made several attempts at the task, but each time I realized that I was going to need lots of assistance.

My lucky day came when my oldest daughter, Wanda, offered to help. She retired in December of 2007 after teaching for 36 years. Though she had no writing experience, she has a master's degree in Reading, so I figured she was the one for the job. For the next year and a half, we both struggled with the task of telling my story - a job that was far larger than either of us had imagined. I know that she got weary a time or two, but she never gave up, and for that I thank her. Without her hard work and determination, this book would never have been written. Without her help, the story of the best bomber crew in World War II would never have been told.

My deep appreciation also goes to Raymond Tucker, Lt. Colonel USAF Retired, (no relation) for his part in motivating and inspiring me to write this book. Over the years, Ray has become quite the expert on the history of the B-17. His interest was initially sparked because his father had been a flight engineer aboard a B-17 and was killed on a training flight.

When I met Ray several years ago and he learned of my World War II experiences, he honored me by presenting me with a model of *Kwiturbitchin* which he had assembled. A photograph of the model of the B-17 and an article about the event was published in the Panama City *News Herald* in August of 2002. I consider myself very fortunate to have been befriended by a man who I consider one of the most knowledgeable B-17 enthusiasts in the country.

- Ken

Introduction

Wanda Tucker Goodwin

As long as I can remember, I've wanted to write; but like so many other aspiring writers, life seemed to get in the way. That was until I retired in December of 2007 after 36 years of teaching. My retirement plan was to pursue my many other interests and also spend quality time with my family. Knowing that my father had always wanted to write his memoir was the perfect avenue to do both.

It seemed to be the ideal situation for an inexperienced writer. My father would provide the material; all I had to do was write it down. How difficult could that be? Well, it turned out to be very difficult; so much so that I almost gave up a time or two. Fortunately, no matter how frustrated I got, I kept reminding myself that my father had never reneged on a promise to me, and I sure wasn't about to do that to him.

At the beginning of this venture, we had a great time. I gained so much insight and added respect for my father as he shared his experiences with me while I operated a tape recorder, took notes and asked questions. The problems began when I had to sit down at the computer with the tape player and try to retell and organize the stories. First of all, I couldn't find my father's voice. No matter how hard I tried, my voice kept telling his stories - that would never do. Somehow, I managed to tune out my voice and pay attention to his; consequently, the writing process went well - for awhile.

As we progressed, so did my imagination. Clearly, I just wanted to make the stories more interesting for the readers. When I finished what I considered a very interesting version of one of my dad's stories, I would read it back to him. Often he would reply, "But that's not how it happened."

My response would be, "Well, it could have happened that way."

"Well, it didn't," was always his reply and, by his tone of voice, I knew that I had better stick to the facts.

So, I was back at the computer rewriting, trying to leave my imagination out of the process. From this venture, I have learned that there lies a fiction writer within me. I found it so difficult to stick to the truth. I enjoyed myself so much more when I tried to sneak in a little fiction.

Probably, the biggest challenge was organizing all the events into a format that flowed and made sense. That was a huge task, but somehow I was able to fit almost all of my dad's memories into a table of contents that I hope will flow and make sense to the readers.

What a learning experience and exciting adventure this has been. Without my dad and his memories of World War II, I would have never discovered that I actually do enjoy writing. Without my dad's story to tell, I doubt that I would have ever been a partner in writing a book, which has always been a dream of mine. Without my dad, I would never have known the excitement and thrill of knowing that I actually helped produce a wonderful memoir that I think people of all ages will enjoy. I hope, too, that as we continue to lose our surviving World War II veterans, our readers will not forget the sacrifices made for us by the greatest generation that ever lived.

Acknowledgements

In the last few years, self publishing has become an easy and popular means for novice writers to get their work "out there." Wendy Woodrick, owner of Priority Publishing Company, has been instrumental in helping my dad and me with this venture. Wendy has been most gracious and has guided us every step of the way. We could never have published this book without her help and guidance.

When self publishing, writers take responsibility for their own editing. Since it is very difficult to edit your own work, and professional editors charge two to three dollars a page, I called on friends for help. All I could offer was a free lunch and a copy of the book, but the response was overwhelming. I was amazed at each individual's perception of editing and was completely overwhelmed at how much I learned from the editors. Each and every editor contributed, in some way, to help make "Last Roll Call" something to be proud of.

Our historical editors were extremely important in making sure all the facts were accurate. Dolores Taranto Roux, an old friend of my father's, is quite the historian for her hometown of Apalachicola, Florida. She was very helpful and was always willing to give of her time and knowledge.

We called upon Raymond Tucker (no relation), a friend of my father's, to make sure all our facts about World War II were accurate. He is quite a historian concerning World War II and has a special interest in the "bomber boys" who flew in the B-17s. It was indeed an honor to have Ray edit our book.

I would also like to thank my father's two surviving siblings, Thelma Rowell and Loyce Novak. They both were happy to share their memories of growing up with my father in East Point, FL. We all had a great time as the three siblings shared experiences and told stories on one another.

My mother, Virginia Tucker, was very helpful with her support and encouragement while we struggled to get this book written. She read all the drafts and played a huge role in convincing me that my writing was good enough to tell my dad's story. The wonderful meals she prepared also helped encourage us to keep working.

My sister, Barbara Tucker, proved to be a first-rate editor. Her expertise seemed to be with sequence of events. Because the stories were so familiar to me, I sometimes lost the reader as I moved from one event to another. She was particularly helpful in pointing that out to me.

Margaret Tidmore, my wonderful friend and neighbor, was always a source of encouragement. She had such positive comments about the book and continued to keep me optimistic about the outcome. She was especially verbal about how parts of the book made her laugh and cry. What more could a writer ask for? Margaret is one of the most patriotic people I know, so it was an honor to have her as an editor.

I'm so grateful for my friends who happily agreed to be unpaid editors. April Bland Vickery, a loyal friend, avid reader, and retired elementary teacher answered my call for help. Thankfully, she had an eye for details and had questions that I never thought about. I so enjoyed her suggestions and comments, written just like a teacher who was trying to encourage an aspiring student.

My friend and past co-worker, Mary Lent, volunteered her expertise as a Language Arts teacher. I very much appreciated her positive comments and suggestions. She did an excellent job in all aspects of editing; however, she seemed to have a knack for catching my many missing and misplaced commas. I'm so grateful for friends who pay attention to punctuation, because I've never been any good at it.

The last editor I would like to thank is Shirley Myers, a wonderful old friend from college. I certainly got lucky when she agreed to be an editor because it turned out that she has a remarkable talent for the task. She, along with the help of her mother, Rhoda, corrected many misspelled words. Shirley actually encouraged and taught me how to use semicolons. I was like a kid with a new toy; consequently, I probably have a record number of semicolons in the book. At her suggestion, I also threw in a colon or two. She also introduced me to the effectiveness of using dashes, which I incorporated a number of times. Thank you, Shirley, for broadening my punctuation horizons.

I have been both encouraged and inspired by my new writing friends at the *Panhandle Writers Guild* and *Writers Aglow*. The writers of both organizations have been most helpful, and I would recommend them to any aspiring writer. The summer visiting author series offered by FSU-Panama City campus also proved to be a great source of knowledge and motivation. Thank you all.

- *Wanda*

Table of Contents

A Mission

Welcomed Changes Off Base

Mishaps, Malfunctions & Maladies

Memorable Missions

Headed Home

Ready, Willing and Able

Chapter 1

Pearl Harbor

Like everyone, the events of December 7, 1941, forever changed my life. After that day I was no longer a carefree young man. At the time, I was only 16 and still in high school; but I knew, I knew I was headed to war. I honestly don't remember being afraid or anxious at the thought of going. What I remember most was the anticipation and excitement during the seemingly endless months that I had to wait. During those months, I was so serious and completely focused on following the war efforts. Nothing was more important to me than being knowledgeable and prepared when it came my time to go.

The Monday after Pearl Harbor, I skipped school to hear the live broadcast when President Roosevelt declared war on Japan. History was being made that day, and I wanted to hear it firsthand. After the broadcast, I looked over at my dad expecting to see his eyes filled with pride and excitement like mine. Instead, I was troubled to see eyes full of sadness and fear looking back at me. Dad had fought in France during World War I, so he knew the truth about war.

The next day, when asked to explain the reason for my absence it became obvious that my principal wasn't impressed. "I would like to have heard it too," he smirked. Then he proceeded to lecture me about "getting my priorities straight." I wanted to tell him that they were.

Pearl Harbor changed everything; now, we had something to talk about other than how tough times were. After

school, I always hung around my dad's seafood business in East Point, Florida. I liked to venture down to the beach where the local fishermen were often busy hanging in a new gill net or mending an old one. I always enjoyed listening to the fishermen talk about the weather, fishing, and the latest local gossip. As expected, after Pearl Harbor, talk quickly turned to the war. "We may be down, but we're not out. Just give us a little time to reorganize and the Japs are gonna wish they had never heard of Pearl Harbor."

War was the topic of conversation around my house and community and even on the daily school bus ride to Carrabelle. Discussions on the topic of war could be heard in every classroom, hallway, and playing field at Carrabelle High School. However, the best place to hear talk about the war was in Apalachicola. Because of my dad's business, he often made trips into town, and I was always eager to ride with him. It never took long for me to find what I was looking for.

Our two main stops in Apalachicola were always the train depot and the Acme Ice Plant. At The Apalachicola Northern Railroad depot, we unloaded our crabmeat and lingered for a brief visit. Dad and I joined in as the workers cussed Hitler and the Japs. They even took stabs at the Russians. "You can't trust those Russians; nobody can predict what they're gonna do."

At the ice plant, I hung around the back of the truck as the workers loaded 300 pound blocks of ice and covered them with tarpaulins. As expected, talk turned to the war. "Let's send our boys over there so the fighting won't be on American soil." I couldn't have agreed more.

Because of Dad's business, he regularly traded at Wefing's Marine Hardware Store. Sometimes he had business next door at Allen's Machine Shop. Often, he would be delayed at the machine shop which gave me the opportunity to take off on my own and explore the town. I was interested in war talk, and it never took me long to find it.

I soon learned that Sangaree's Barber Shop was about the best place in town to hang around if you wanted to hear

what the locals were saying about the war. You didn't even have to get a haircut if you didn't need one. Back in those days, the barber shop was a busy place. Many customers, often local older gentlemen, visited almost daily for a shave. It seemed that everybody had an opinion on what it would take to win the war. After listening to some heated discussions, I became quite concerned. If some of those old men were right, the war might be over before I had a chance to get there. "If the Russians join up with us, the Germans are done for."

All over town there was a lot of talk about the Apalachicola National Guard Unit that had already been deployed to the Territory of Alaska to defend the coast and the Aleutian Islands from the Japanese. So many names of sons, fathers, and brothers were spoken by concerned relatives and friends. There was talk about other local men who were already fighting in Europe and Asia. Some of the names I recognized as cousins and friends. I particularly remember a cousin, Keith Bloodsworth, who was in The Marine Corp 5th Division fighting on Guadalcanal. While I was in high school, my brother and I corresponded with him on a regular basis.

I could only hope that one day some local guy sitting in the barber chair might say, "You heard about that Tucker boy from East Point? Hear tell he's a fighter pilot."

On our way home from Apalachicola, Dad always stopped at Gorrie Station. It was kind of a gas station and tavern up on Hwy. 98 on a bluff overlooking the Apalachicola Bay and the Gorrie Bridge to Apalach. The locals stopped at the station to buy gas and drink beer, as well as talk about the weather, fishing, and the war. We always made a quick stop for Dad to pick up his subscription to the Florida Times Union. He subscribed to the Jacksonville newspaper because he thought it had the best coverage of the war.

During our brief stop at the station, I would linger for awhile and listen to the men chitchat, but I knew I couldn't waste too much time if I wanted to have a look at the many newspapers left laying around on the bar. I'd pull up a stool, spread out the papers, and devour the headlines and photographs. If Dad tarried awhile, I had time to read some of the articles which I would discuss with him on the ride home.

My family was fortunate to own a radio which quickly became the latest source of war information. We listened to radio *WFLA* out of Gainesville and *WSUN* out of St. Petersburg. At night, we could pick up a station out of New Orleans and another out of Cincinnati. Together, Dad and I listened to the war broadcasts. After we were certain we had heard all the latest war news, we would tune in to some beautiful classical music as we listened to *The Sunday Night Firestone Hour* and *The Bell Telephone Hour*.

Those were special times, just my dad and me sitting around the radio. Though we had always been close, the war would bind us in a strange way, not just father to son but man to man. Long after all us kids were in bed, I can remember hearing the soft hum of the voices of the newscasters as Dad sat up late into the night.

By far, the most thrilling source of information about the war came from the newsreels at the Dixie Theater in Apalachicola. A trip into town to see a show at the Dixie was a real treat, topped only by the thrill of getting to see and hear the actual war footage up on that huge screen. I watched, with much anticipation, as the ground troops trudged through the endless mud and snow. I was in awe of the dashing and brave young pilots as they manned their planes and took off for the dangerous skies. There was no doubt in my mind that I wanted to be a pilot, and those newsreels made me even more sure of my decision. As I sat there in the darkness, I could hardly contain my excitement and the pride I felt in knowing that I would be over there soon, but even tomorrow wouldn't be soon enough.

I don't remember exactly where I developed my interest in flying. It probably began at an early age when Dad told stories about his experiences in World War I. He fought on the ground in France, but he told stories about watching dogfights up over the lines. Those tales sparked my interest, so I started reading about the World War I Flying Aces. The Germans,

French, Americans, British; they all had some. I remember way back, reading about Capt. Eddie Rickenbacker being America's leading Ace. Whenever I had to write essays or reports in school, I always chose some sort of aviation as my topic.

This photo of my father was taken in 1918 while serving in the Army in France during WWI.

Arthur L. Tucker, Sr.

That's me when I was about eight with my aviator goggles and helmet. Next to me are my sisters Thelma, Dattie and Hilda and our family dog, Fritzie.

Chapter 2

Apalachicola

Because there were no stores in East Point, trips to Apalachicola were necessary, not only for my father's business, but for supplies for the family. Our trips usually included a stop or two at one of the many shops lining the busy streets. We always made a stop at The Swanee Grocery Store or the A & P to pick up our staples which seemed to mostly consist of: flour, coffee, lard, a few canned goods and dried beans. The Russells had a meat market in the back of The Swanee. Occasionally, Dad would buy a piece of beef - now that was a real treat.

Times were tough for all the shopkeepers. Dad and I always chuckled when we passed one particular small grocery store that was a few blocks from the main part of town. The owner was known to swindle customers out of a little extra cash. We would both look in the window, and sure enough, there was the broom leaning up by the register. When unsuspecting customers checked out, he would add the price of the broom to their ticket. If anybody caught the extra charge, the owner would point to the broom and tell them he thought it was theirs. He got away with that for years. There's no telling how much money he made off that one broom.

There were two drug stores in Apalach at that time; Buzzett's and Creekmore's. We often stopped in for supplies my mom needed for home doctoring. I remember picking up Groves chill tonic, Epsom salt, Caster oil and Vick's salve. You didn't have to have a prescription for paregoric, but you did have to sign for it because it had opium in it. Back then, you

only went to a doctor as a last resort or if you were rich.

If you stepped on a nail or cut yourself, somebody would pour kerosene on the wound. Turpentine would work too. The same was true if you got finned by a catfish or took a hit from a stingray. It must have worked because I don't remember anybody getting lockjaw or gangrene.

The Bowery was an area of town down by the train station where Demo George and the Nichole's family each had general stores. I loved going in those stores because there was so much to look at. What a luxury it must have been to go in the store, pick out the clothes you wanted, try them on, pay, and take your merchandise home all in the same day.

Most of our clothes were ordered from Sears Roebuck or Montgomery Ward. Seems like we had to wait weeks for the package to come in, and even after that we often had to wait until my dad had the money to pay for it. Back then you could order things cash on delivery (COD). You actually paid for the package when it came in at the post office. Whenever my dad noticed a man out oystering late in the day or on Sunday, he would nod toward the fella and comment, "He must have a package at the post office."

Down on The Bowery there was a little place called The Candy Kitchen. I remember admiring all the pretty colors and strong, sweet smells. It didn't cost anything to look and drool. Often, Dad would go in The Riverside Café to get a cup of coffee. Occasionally, he would surprise me with a doughnut for the trip home. I would slowly savor every bite; however, all traces of the rare treat had to be consumed before we reached home and the watchful eyes of my sisters.

Even back then, Apalachicola had the reputation of being a historical port town. Before Pearl Harbor, I had never been particularly interested in exploring the history of the town. But now, because I knew I was destined to become part of history, I decided I should learn about the history that existed right here near my hometown; so, whenever I got the chance, I ventured out to see what I could learn about the historical old town of Apalachicola.

A stroll down the river front could be a history lesson in itself. Warehouses were still standing where cotton was exchanged before the Civil War. During that time, Apalachicola became one of the largest cotton ports in the United States. Images of paddle wheelers and steamboats crowding the docks easily came to mind - what a place Apalachicola must have been when cotton was king.

As a boy, I remember a paddle wheeler making a stop in Apalach on its weekly run. It seems like the festive event was on Thursdays. With much anticipation, the townspeople gathered to see who and what would be loaded on and off the boat before returning upriver. People on the boat were dressed up real fancy like I had never seen. Once, I spied a little boy and girl probably about five and six. They were so dressed up in fancy clothes that at first I thought they were dolls. How in the world they could even move in those stiff clothes was a wonder to me.

A stroll down to Scipio Creek reminded me that the timber industry had once been huge along The Apalachicola River. As a kid, I remember walking down to the creek, looking across at Shipe's sawmill, and listening to the whining and screeching sounds of the saws. If the breeze blew in my direction, I could smell the fresh cut timber. To this day, I still enjoy the smell of fresh-milled lumber. Back then, on a calm, clear day, we could hear the mill whistle all the way across the bay in East Point.

At one time, there had been a huge sponge trade among the Greeks in Apalachicola. The trade extended as far east as Carrabelle. There was no evidence left that I ever found - just talk. According to the locals, the sponges just dried up in the area and the divers moved further south to Tarpon Springs. I always intended to visit Tarpon Springs and see what it was all about.

Apalachicola had always been famous for its oysters. Really, all of Franklin County was in the oyster business. Dad mostly dealt in crabmeat, but he also handled fish, shrimp and oysters. I remember walking down Water Street, in Apalach, and seeing oyster shells piled as high as a two-story building.

There would be so many piles it looked like a small mountain range, and when the sun bleached them white, it looked like mountains covered in snow. After the rain washed away some of the oyster mud and the sun dried up some of the stink, kids enjoyed climbing and playing on those huge mounds of shells. It was kind of a badge-of-honor thing, among the boys, to see just who was tough enough to play on those shell piles bare-footed.

Apalachicola's historical claim to fame had to be the invention of the ice machine. The event happened in the 1850s at the Marine Hospital where Dr. John Gorrie was attempting to find a way to cool the air for his patients with malaria and yellow fever. I don't remember there being any markers or monuments when I was a kid, but we all knew about the great invention because we studied about Dr. Gorrie in Florida History. Many years later, probably in the 1950s, a museum was built with a replica of his invention; also, a monument was erected marking his burial site.

I soon became more interested in the people than the places. The large population of Greeks and Italians fascinated me. They had the most interesting and musical sounding names like Lichardello, Sangaree, Zingarelli, Messina and Taranto. I enjoyed listening to them talk to each other in their native language. Some of the Italians were loud and boisterous and gestured dramatically with their hands. One of my mother's brothers fit that description. The shopkeepers were often Greek, and the Italians mostly worked in the seafood business. My father had lots of Italian friends along the waterfront.

My mother's grandparents had been fishermen in Sicily, so I felt a particular bond with the Italians. Their name was *Segari* but was changed to Segree shortly after they arrived in New Orleans just before the Civil War. Because of my olive skin and dark hair, I seemed to fit right in. I was thrilled when, one day, an Italian fisherman asked me to help carry a heavy net to his boat. From his gesturing, I could tell what he wanted, so I happily obliged. While he carried on in Italian all the way down to the dock, I just kept smiling and nodding; he never knew I wasn't one of them.

I wasn't actually there, but I did hear an interesting story concerning my foreign friends. It was early in the war when the Italians joined forces with the Germans and invaded Greece. The story goes that a local Italian visited a coffee shop owned by a Greek. The Greek owner had just learned about his country's takeover and was not happy to see an Italian come in his shop. Supposedly, the irate owner grabbed a pot of coffee and chased the bewildered Italian customer out of the shop.

Chapter 3

My Family

My father owned and operated A. L. Tucker Seafood, a wholesale business dealing mostly in crabmeat. In the early 1930s he had been the first dealer in Florida to pack crabmeat in cans for the northern retail markets. He started out selling crabmeat in peanut butter jars to the locals around East Point and Apalachicola.

It was Dad's lucky day when the owner of the Steel and Tin Product Company in Baltimore stopped by and bought some crab meat. His company produced cans for the vegetable industry. The owner saw a business opportunity and offered to design a can that would hold one pound of crabmeat. Even though my dad had no money, they shook hands and the guy sent 250 cans on a trial basis. He even found a market for the crabmeat right there in Baltimore. The cans worked great, and so began a lifelong business agreement and friendship.

I often helped my dad pack up the crabmeat for shipment. The cans were packed into barrels that were made at the barrel factory right there in Apalach. I remember watching an old black man form up the barrels. The best I remember, we bought one of three sizes: lime, flour or sugar, depending on the size of the shipment. We'd ice down the cans real good and cover the top of the barrel with burlap for the trip to Columbus, Georgia where the barrels were transferred to a refrigerated car.

I remember my father as a hard-working family man who was well thought of in our small community. He was

A. L. Tucker's Wholesale Seafood Company, East Point, FL around 1943. That's my dad's old '38 Dodge pick-up.

known as a man of few words; consequently, when he spoke, people listened.

Arthur L. Tucker, Sr. died in 1956 at the age of 67 of heart failure. He smoked Prince Albert and rolled his own. Many times I tried to get him to quit, not because I was concerned about his health, but because I was concerned about the money. When I was probably about 14, I went so far as to ask him how many cans a week he smoked and how much a can cost. After doing the math, I informed him, "Dad, you're burning up $76 a year. You've gotta quit." He promised to cut back, and I'm sure he tried to quit, but he had been smoking since he was 13 and just couldn't do it.

When I think of my mother, I remember a woman who never stopped. Before she married, she had been a teacher in a one-room schoolhouse near East Point. During her married life, she looked after the needs of six kids, maintained a large garden, and cared for several chickens and a milk cow. Daily, she helped my dad in the crab house. Sometimes she picked, but mostly she weighed up the cans of fresh picked crab meat and prepared them for shipment. At the end of the day she washed down the picking tables with Clorox before she came home to fix supper. The smell of Clorox always seemed to mingle with the flavors of whatever was on the table. To this day, whenever I smell Clorox, I think of my mother.

My mom was an avid church goer and regularly attended the little Methodist church in East Point where she played the piano. She was often called upon to help deliver babies and was always willing to help out other families in need. As a child, I remember wondering if she ever slept.

My mother, Camelia Segree Tucker, died in 1990 at the age of 93. She had been a widow for over 30 years but managed to maintain the large family home where she died. In her later years, she was fortunate to have children and grandchildren nearby to help look after her. Up until the last few years of her life, when she broke a hip, she was able to attend church and go fishing up the creeks - her two favorite activities. In her later years, nothing made her happier than for some of the kids to come by and pick her up, grunt up a can of worms, load the cane poles and head for Casher's Creek or Whisky George Creek to catch a mess of bream, blue gills or stump knockers.

The oldest child and my only brother, Arthur, was a junior so all his life he was called Arthur Boy. Because of a childhood injury, he spent many of his school age years at the Florida Crippled Children's Home in Umatilla. I was eight and he was twelve when he accidently hit himself in the shin with an ax. The site developed a bad bruise and got infected. Dr. Dykes, from Carrabelle, came to the house for about a month and treated Arthur, but the infection got worse. The doctor sent Arthur to St. Luke's hospital in Jacksonville, and from there, he was sent to Umatilla where he was diagnosed with osteomyelitis, a bone infection.

Then there were my four sisters: Hilda, Thelma, Dattie and Loyce. They seemed to spend most of their time with their friends and girl cousins huddled together giggling about something. I didn't have much time to spend with them because I had so many chores to do, being the only boy left at home.

My mother, Camelia Segree Tucker, before she married my father. The picture was made probably about 1918.

The Stamps contained in this Book are valid only after the lawful holder of this Book has signed the certificate below, and are void if detached contrary to the Regulations. (A father, mother, or guardian may sign the name of a person under 18.) In case of questions, difficulties, or complaints, consult your local Ration Board.

Certificate of Book Holder

I, *the undersigned*, do hereby certify that I have observed all the conditions and regulations governing the issuance of this War Ration Book; that the "Description of Book Holder" contained herein is correct; that an application for issuance of this book has been duly made by me or on my behalf; and that the statements contained in said application are true to the best of my knowledge and belief.

Kenneth S. Tucker [Book Holder's Own Name]
(Signature of, or on behalf of, Book Holder)

Any person signing on behalf of Book Holder must sign his or her own name below and indicate relationship to Book Holder Arthur L. Tucker

Father
(Father, Mother, or Guardian)

OPA Form No. R-302

UNITED STATES OF AMERICA

War Ration Book One

No. 510964 -306

WARNING

1 Punishments ranging as high as *Ten Years' Imprisonment or $10,000 Fine, or Both*, may be imposed under United States Statutes for violations thereof arising out of infractions of Rationing Orders and Regulations.

2 This book must not be transferred. It must be held and used only by or on behalf of the person to whom it has been issued, and anyone presenting it thereby represents to the Office of Price Administration, an agency of the United States Government, that it is being so held and so used. For any misuse of this book it may be taken from the holder by the Office of Price Administration.

3 In the event either of the departure from the United States of the person to whom this book is issued, or his or her death, the book must be surrendered in accordance with the Regulations.

4 Any person finding a lost book must deliver it promptly to the nearest Ration Board.

OFFICE OF PRICE ADMINISTRATION

Ration card issued to me when I was 17.

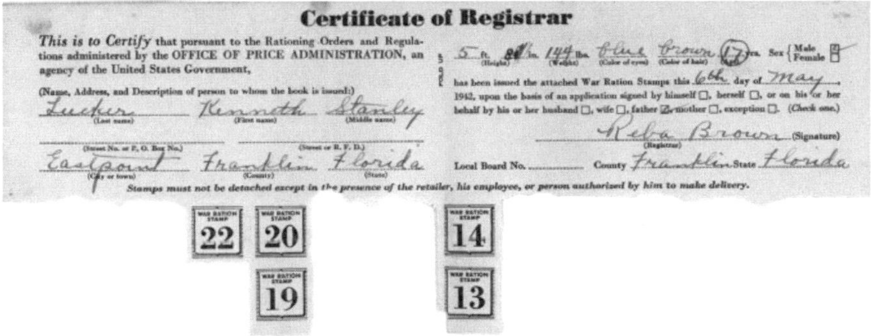

Certificate of Registrar

This is to Certify that pursuant to the Rationing Orders and Regulations administered by the OFFICE OF PRICE ADMINISTRATION, an agency of the United States Government,

(Name, Address, and Description of person to whom the book is issued:)

Tucker (Last name) Kenneth (First name) Stanley (Middle name)

(Street No. or P. O. Box No.) (Street or R. F. D.)

Eastpoint (City or town) Franklin (County) Florida (State)

5 ft. 8 in. (Height) 144 lbs. (Weight) blue (Color of eyes) brown (Color of hair) 17 yrs. Sex {Male ☒ Female ☐}

has been issued the attached War Ration Stamps this 6th day of May, 1942, upon the basis of an application signed by himself ☐, herself ☐, or on his or her behalf by his or her husband ☐, wife ☐, father ☒, mother ☐, exception ☐. (Check one.)

Reba Brown (Signature) (Registrar)

Local Board No. ______ County Franklin State Florida

Stamps must not be detached except in the presence of the retailer, his employee, or person authorized by him to make delivery.

The inside of my ration card with stamps.

I was very happy and proud to see my family doing all we could to help with the war efforts. We did the best we could with our ration cards and were always willing to help out other families who never seemed to have enough food and supplies. Because Dad produced food for the public, he was entitled to more than the usual ration of gasoline which was two gallons a week. My family never went hungry, but we sure did eat a lot of mullet and beans. Even today, fried mullet and lima beans remain one of my favorite meals, maybe with the addition of a little coleslaw.

Talking about mullet and beans and hard times brings to mind a song that my nephew, Billy Samford, recently wrote. Billy plays the banjo with a bluegrass band from Wakulla and Leon County called *Coon Bottom Creek*. Billy, the youngest child of my sister Dattie, grew up hearing tales about how hard times were during the Depression and how his grandfather worked so hard to provide for his family. Billy never knew my

dad; he died before Billy was born. Billy told me that he wrote this song as a humble tribute to his grandfather. Please read Billy's tribute titled *Cold Biscuits* at the end of this book.

If Dad ever got wind of any black-market dealings going on, he made every effort to curtail the activity. I remember one old farmer from Alabama who tried to sell my dad a bucket of lard, which was a ration item. The farmer had added a little pork rind to the lard and was selling it as pork. Dad convinced the Alabama farmer to head for the state line and never come back.

Times were tough, but when I think back on my childhood, other than my brother's injury, mostly I remember a close-knit family who made the most of any situation. I flashback to times spent, as a family, sitting on the porch listening to the radio. The rest of the family would join Dad and me on Saturday nights to listen to the *Grand Ole Opry*. We enjoyed and laughed along with *George Burns and Gracie Allen*. Other family favorites were *Amos and Andy* and *Lum and Abner*.

It was funny to me how everybody sat real still and stared at the radio like the actual people were right there talking and singing. I got a lot more out of the broadcasts if I watched the reactions and expressions on everybody's faces. If I looked away from the radio and at the listener's faces, that old front porch sure seemed to come alive.

Many young men joined the Armed Forces at 17 if their parents would give consent; others lied about their age. As bad as I wanted to go, I knew I could better serve my country if I graduated first; besides, my parents would have never agreed to let me go before I graduated. During the year and a half that I had to wait, I kept up with the war by reading newspapers and listening to radio broadcasts. While I waited, I did what I could to help out with the local war efforts and to prepare myself to someday defend our great country.

I figured it wouldn't hurt to get a head start on my training, so I signed up for a correspondence course I had seen advertised in a magazine I subscribed to called *Popular Aviation*. The course was very enlightening because it familiarized me

with the development of all kinds of aircraft and engines; it was a real good indoctrination into aviation. I particularly paid attention to the fighters and bombers that were being used overseas. After I completed the course, I had no doubt, that with just a little hands-on training, I could fly any one of those magnificent aircraft.

During my senior year, I was thrilled when the Shop teacher told us our assignment was to assemble model airplanes that would be used by the Armed Forces in aircraft recognition training. After they were put together, we painted them and glued on the insignias. The scaled models were authentic, and no two were the same. I remember the one I assembled was a British twin-engine light bomber called a Beaufort.

The summer between my junior and senior year, I worked as a carpenter's helper at the Apalachicola Army Air Field. The site was to be an auxiliary field for Tyndall Air Force Base out of Panama City. My cousin, Tonnar Segree, had an old truck, so he gave several of the East Point locals a ride to work. The project was in the beginning stages, so I helped build barracks. I learned some useful skills that summer and went on to enjoy carpentry work the rest of my life.

Chapter 4

German Subs in the Gulf

There was talk of German submarines in the area; consequently, at night the Coast Guard patrolled St. George Island on horseback. St. George is a barrier island four miles off the coast of East Point. Dad must not have been too concerned because we gill netted for mullet all around the bay side of the island. Often we came ashore at night and built a fire while we waited for the tide to turn. We never ventured over to the Gulf side so we never encountered the Coast Guard. To my knowledge, no German subs were ever sighted off St. George nor did any German terrorist row ashore in rubber rafts.

There was, however, a German submarine disaster a few miles to the west of St. George Island off the coast of Apalachicola. A couple of local fishermen had reported seeing a submarine in the area, but nobody believed them. That was, until one night in the summer of 1942 when the British tanker, the *Empire Mica*, exploded offshore. Talk was, the explosion could be heard on the coast over 20 miles away. Residents of Apalachicola rushed out to the scene and rescued the few survivors. Those fortunate sailors were taken to the Armory where local women were waiting to care for them. A local merchant donated clothes and several residents invited the survivors to be guests in their homes until they were strong enough to travel. In later interviews, the survivors talked about how well they were treated by the fine people of Apalachicola.

Because of the threat of German submarines in the area, a local German fisherman was ordered to stay off the water at

night. One night he tied up to a beacon in the middle of the bay and spent the night on his boat. Evidently, he was being watched because the authorities were waiting for him when he got to the dock the next morning. As a result, he was no longer allowed on the water at all. The man was a fisherman and had no other means to support his family. He started hauling dirt and wood and somehow managed to make a living. The incident was never made public; only a few people in East Point ever knew about it.

Chapter 5

Eighteen and Ready to Go

Finally, in May of '43 I turned eighteen and graduated from high school. Dad couldn't get me over to Apalach fast enough to register with the local draft board and volunteer for service. The head of the Draft Board was a seasoned, old fellow by the name of Capt. Farley Warren. The Captain liked to help out the volunteers and told me I would be hearing from him soon.

The long and frustrating wait was almost over, and I knew that I was about to begin the adventure of a lifetime. I had no doubt that I would soon be joining forces with other young men who would unite to defend our great country; history was being made and I was going to be part of it.

All that was left to do was wait for my letter to arrive. I had never been fond of working in the crab house, but now I didn't mind. I was a short timer, and besides, I needed something to do to help pass the time. Most people think crab meat is a delicious delicacy; but not me. Nothing stinks worse in this world than the steam from cooking crabs. Imagine combining that disgusting stink with the

Carrabelle High School, Class of 1943.

sweltering heat. To this day I still gag at the smell of cooking crabs.

When the planes from Tyndall Army-Air Field flew over during training missions, everybody would run out on the dock to admire them. During one fly over, my two younger sisters, Loyce and Dattie, happened to be out on the dock. I was very proud of them when they both stood at attention with their hands over their hearts as they sang at the top of their lungs, *Off we go into the wild blue yonder…* Watching them made me even more anxious to be up there flying one of those fighters and not down on the ground shoveling stinking crabs.

After three months of waiting and working in the crab house, I decided to pay another visit to the draft board to see what the holdup was. The old captain seemed to like the idea that I was tired of waiting, and that I was past ready to go. He also liked the fact that, on my own, I had taken the aviation correspondence course. He knew he had the makings of a pilot standing in front of him, and he wanted to get me on my way. Somebody else would have to cook and clean stinking crabs. I was needed in the air wars over Europe or the Pacific.

On August 20, 1943, just a few days after my visit with Captain Warren, I was standing with four other guys in front of the court house in Apalachicola about to board a Trailways bus. Though I was obviously the youngest of the group, the old captain put me in charge. What a thrill it was for me to call out each guy's name and hand him his orders. I got a big kick out of giving the command for everyone to board the bus. Never before in my life had I felt so grown up and important. I couldn't wait to be a real military officer. The best part of all was that my dad was watching. When that bus pulled away, I could see him leaning up against his old truck as he waved goodbye.

APPOINTMENT OF LEADER OR ASSISTANT LEADER

OFFICE OF THE DIRECTOR OF SELECTIVE SERVICE
WASHINGTON

To Whom It May Concern:

Special confidence being placed in the integrity and ability of

___**** KENNETH STANLEY TUCKER ****___

he is hereby appointed {leader / ~~assistant leader~~} of a contingent of selected men from Local

Board No. I of FRANKLIN County, in the State

of FLORIDA

He is, therefore, charged with the enforcement of the Selective Service Regulations governing selected men enroute to Induction Stations during the journey from

APALACHICOLA, FLA. to CAMP BLANDING, FLA.

and all men included within the contingent are directed to obey his lawful orders during the journey.

By Order of the Director of Selective Service

Date AUGUST 20,1943.

J P Hinley
Chairman of Local Board.

D. S. S. Form 158

10—18047

Testing and Training

Chapter 6

Camp Blanding, Florida
Induction & Swearing In

It was an uneventful bus ride to Camp Blanding, just outside of Stark, near Jacksonville. The other enlistees were quiet and well-behaved so I was able to sit back and enjoy the ride. Mainly, I thought about how the adventure I had been dreaming about for so long was finally happening. At last, I was on my way - but to where?

We arrived at Blanding, filed off the bus, and were escorted into a large auditorium filled with a bunch of nervous looking civilians, just like us. The guys in uniforms, the ones shouting out directions, stood out like beacons in the crowd of bewildered civilians. The beacons directed us to one of the many lines for in-processing where we were asked endless questions.

"Aviation Cadet's, Sir," of course, was my answer when asked which branch of service I wanted.

"So you want to be a hotshot pilot?" was the response I got from the cocky sergeant.

My simple reply was, "I just want to be a pilot, Sir."

During that short stay at Camp Blanding, I had my first ever physical, which was also my first experience with running around naked in front of other men and peeing in a bottle. I was so relieved when my eyesight tested perfect. My hearing was fine as well as my depth perception. My teeth were in great shape even though I had never been to a dentist. Not a single cavity; guess it was all the seafood and beans.

There were lots of written and physical tests, which I passed with no problems. Then we were back on the bus headed home. On the return trip there were only four of us; one of the original four guys from Apalachicola had already been sent back home with a case of latent syphilis.

We were given 21 days at home to "get our affairs in order." I was 18 years old, so the only affair I had to get in order was having as much fun as possible. Dad had already hired another houseman to take my place at the crab house, so my time was my own.

A lot of my leave time was spent at the Brown's tennis court down on the Point. The Brown family had tried to start kind of a resort with bath houses, tennis courts and a skating rink. It didn't go over too well, so it quickly became a gathering place for the Brown's children and their friends. I never did take to skating, but I learned to love tennis and got pretty good at it. In fact, I was playing tennis at the Browns the day my dad came down and told us that the Japs had bombed Pearl Harbor.

That's me on the left, then my cousins John Williams and Oliver Segree, my brother Arthur and Ben Brown at the Brown's tennis court at East Point.

My fondest memories of those days were the beach parties at Lagoon Beach. Dad would let Arthur, my brother, and me borrow his old '35 Ford truck. We'd load up with our friends, my two oldest sisters, Hilda and Thelma, and their friends. The gang would head west through Apalachicola and follow the highway along the coast for several miles. McNeil's Store was our first stop to buy snacks and drinks and then on down to the beach to build a huge bonfire.

On our way home, we would pass through Apalach late at night. Without fail, we would pull in by the back door of Thompson's Bakery. Somebody would run and knock on the door and return to the car with a loaf of the hottest, best smelling, best tasting bread you could ever imagine. We would pull big hunks off and have that loaf devoured before we got to the bridge.

Another gathering place was a swimming hole down by the old ferry dock in East Point. The deep hole was dug to accommodate the ferry before there was a bridge to Apalachicola. The area was great for sunbathing, swimming, and diving. If we couldn't get to Lagoon Beach, we would sometimes build bonfires down there at night. The best I remember, the bridge was built in '35. I do remember going over to Apalach on the ferry with Dad when I was a little boy. Bet there aren't very many folks left out there today who can say that.

There must have been lots of good movies out at that time because I remember going to the Dixie quite a few times before I left. Back then, we didn't say we were going to the *movie*, we said we were going to the *picture show*. I can't remember the movies but I sure do remember those newsreels.

After I had "gotten my affairs in order," I once again boarded a Trailways bus in Apalachicola and was headed back to Camp Blanding. The goodbyes were for real this time because there was a chance I would not be coming home again until after my tour of duty. My family, of course, was sad, but, at the same time, they were excited for me because they knew how long I had been waiting and preparing for that moment. Only my dad knew what really lay ahead for me.

As the bus passed through East Point and headed toward Carrabelle, I began to think about another bus ride I had taken this way so many times. All my life, I had ridden a school bus the 15 miles between East Point and Carrabelle. The bus had been filled with my sisters, cousins, and friends. Mostly, the memories were pleasant and reassuring. I thought of my four sisters and the many hours we spent together on that old school bus. What came to mind was how they seemed to always be picking on me or teasing me about some girl who supposedly had a crush on me.

The fond memories of those many bus rides were clouded by one incident that helped shape me into the man I was to become. My memory lapsed back to the fall when I started fifth or sixth grade. That summer I had a really bad case of malaria and was in bed for weeks. The doctor gave me so much quinine my ears still ring to this day. When school started back, I was weak and frail. I had always pretty much kept to myself and was kind of scrappy, so the bullies usually left me alone. But now, because they could, two of them would corner me, wrestle me to the ground and hold me down until I was exhausted from the struggle. Evidently, they considered their little feat to be quality entertainment and double teamed me quite often; however, their days were numbered.

Gradually, my strength began to return, and I was able to catch up on my usual summer job of gathering beach wood for the old iron heaters at home and down at the crab house. I had a two-wheel cart, a one man cross-cut saw and an ax. After school and on weekends, I combed the beach and gathered cart loads of driftwood and washed up logs. Every week my muscles grew stronger as I sawed, chopped, and tugged. I had to be patient, but when I was certain my muscles were strong again, I took both of those losers down. I waited until I knew the time was right; they sure were surprised, but I wasn't.

As the bus passed Carrabelle High School more memories flooded my mind. Again, most all were good. I enjoyed all my classes, especially History and had always made decent grades. Probably the best memory of high school for me was

playing football. The coach told me if I had been a few pounds heavier and a little faster I could have been an all star because I had the skill and agility and a love for the game. During my senior year, I was team captain. I was also quite the track star. My junior year I broke the pole-vault record for Carrabelle High School. I also broke the pole and they didn't get another one.

After passing through Carrabelle and into Lanark, we approached Camp Gordon Johnson where over one hundred-thousand soldiers were being trained. I remembered some of the soldiers who had come up to the school my senior year and helped coach the football team. Bunches of them would attend our home games and root for us just like they had grown up right there with us.

I thought about some of the boys who had come to our house to visit because they were sweet on my two oldest sisters. If they were nice guys and I liked them, I would take them out in the bay to do a little fishing or just out for a boat ride. I liked talking to them about their training and where it would take them.

After leaving Camp Gordon Johnson, the coastline kept me company for many miles. When we turned northward and I caught the last glimpse of the bay, I suddenly felt a terrible loneliness. That coastline had been my constant companion all my life, and leaving it was like saying goodbye to part of my family.

The second trip to Blanding was also a short one. We were sworn in, still in civilian clothes; then we were issued our uniforms and dog tags. I wouldn't wear civilian clothes again for over two years. In fact, to assure that we didn't, we had to mail our civvies home.

After we got our uniforms, it was time to learn how to make up a cot military style. A sergeant set up a cot outside one of the barracks and instructed us all to gather around. We learned about hospital corners and tucking everything in real

tight. He also showed us how to take our second blanket and use it for a dust cover for the exposed sheets and pillow. I never had an inspection officer flip a coin on the beds to see if it bounced, but I heard that some did.

Now that we were sworn in, it was time to start on some serious testing. We were given the Army General Classification Test (AGCT) which was the Army's version of an IQ test. Back then, the Army depended on that test to make initial decisions on what branch of services guys were best suited for. Anybody hoping to go on to cadet training had to do really well on that test. Because of that, we lost quite a few cadet hopefuls.

Chapter 7

Keesler Army Air Field
Biloxi, Mississippi
Cadet Basic Training

In no time at all I was aboard a train headed for Biloxi, Mississippi. What a thrill because that was my first-ever train ride and my first venture out wearing my uniform. Civilians looked at us with such admiration and respect, and I enjoyed that immensely. I had never been much of a ladies' man; but in that uniform, I felt pretty confident. I even got a few smiles from some pretty girls - I was delighted!

In September of 1943, I arrived at Kessler Field, Mississippi, for 13 weeks of cadet-basic training. Our training schedule was so rigid that we were not allowed a single pass. And train we did, in spite of the heat. Most of us were from the southeast so we were used to the heat and humidity, but there was a group of guys from Connecticut who just couldn't take it. They were falling out from the heat so bad that, at one time, drilling on the field was suspended for a week.

My first picture made in uniform while in Basic Training at Keesler Field.

I remember one particular incident when we were marching to the drill field. All was well until some fool in the formation whistled at a captain's wife as they walked by. The furious captain ordered us to stop and put on our gas masks. He ordered the drill sergeant to make sure we wore them all the way to the drill field. Guess he figured it would be hard to whistle at anybody's wife with our mouths covered up. Those masks intensified the already unbearable heat and made it even more difficult to breathe in the sweltering air. We never found out who did the whistling, but you can bet it never happened again.

There were more written tests, just more in depth this time. Quite a few guys were weeded out because they couldn't pass some of the tests. That happened to a friend of mine from Blountstown. He had two years at the University of Florida and seemed to be a real smart guy. For whatever reason, he failed one of the tests. He told the instructor he didn't understand the directions. As expected, he got no sympathy and was told that was part of taking the test. In no time at all, he was sent off for reclassification. He was a real nice guy, and I hated to see him go.

Keesler Field was where I had my first beer. On that particular day, it was so hot on the drill field that we were dismissed and told to walk back to our tents rather than march back in formation. One of my buddies suggested that we stop by a beer garden at the service club and have a "cool one." I don't remember what brand, just that it was ice cold and probably the most refreshing and satisfying drink I had ever had. So began my lifelong enjoyment of a "cool one." From that day on, I only wanted an ice-cold beer when I was hot and sweaty from working or playing out in the heat.

While I was at the beer garden enjoying my first beer, a guy walked up to me and said the usual, "I know you from somewhere." Turned out, it was a kid I had gone to school with in Carrabelle from first grade to about seventh when he moved away. His name was Robert Coker. I never saw him again, but it sure was good to see a familiar face and talk to somebody from home.

Chapter 8

State Teachers College
Morehead, Minnesota
Accelerated College Training Program

Basic training was cut short after just seven weeks and, once again, I was boarding a train. It was November of '43, and we were headed for Morehead State Teachers College in Minnesota. That would be my first experience on a troop train full of nothing but soldiers. I was amazed at how much fun everybody seemed to be having even though conditions were cramped and noisy. No matter how crowded, there always seemed to be room for a crap game. You could count on running up on a bunch of guys down on their knees in the aisle rolling dice or a group of guys gathered around playing poker. Didn't seem to matter who was winning or losing, just that everybody was having a real good time.

I remember looking out over all the young, happy faces and wondering where they would all end up and knowing full well that many of them would not make it back. But at that moment in time, it appeared I was the only one thinking about the future. All the other soldiers were living for the moment - while they still could.

It wasn't a bad trip. We had Pullman cars but not enough sleepers for everybody. I managed to get a bed, probably because I chose not to stay up half the night gambling away what little bit of money I had. I was quite content to lay in my bed and read by the light of a little lamp. The curtain was

closed and I felt very comfortable and safe as the rocking of the train lulled me to sleep. I remember thinking; I'm not hungry, thirsty, dirty, wet, cold, hot, scared, wounded, exhausted, lonely, bored, stressed, or angry. I, too, was living for the moment.

In the accelerated program at Morehead, we were told that we would get the equivalent of two years college in just six months. We would be taking basic courses like English, Math, Physics, History, Geography & Weather and Political Science. Of course, there would be the usual military and physical training.

I wasn't worried about going to cold country; after all, I was from north Florida. I had experienced plenty of cold nights out mullet fishing with my dad in February with a stiff north wind blowing. I remember one winter the tide pools around the bay froze. All of us kids got out there and slid around a little, pretending we were ice skating. Mostly we slid around on our butts. But none of that came close to comparing to the cold I felt when, one night on guard duty, the temperature at the main gate dropped to 30° below zero.

The Army pretty much took over the college. We lived in the dorms which, by Army standards, were pretty nice. Regular students could still attend, but they had to live in town. We were not allowed to look at or speak to any civilians on campus, nor were we allowed to talk in the dining hall. On Saturday afternoons, we were allowed to go into town; on Sundays, we had the day off to do whatever.

Apalachicola Times

Our Boys and Girls in Service

by Capt. J.F. Warren

Kenneth Stanley Tucker, age 18, of East Point has arrived at State Teachers College, Moorehead Minnesota, in the first phase of aircrew training with the army air forces. He will take a course of specialized academic training, elementary flying, and military indoctrination for a period lasting five months. Upon successful completion of that rigorous course, he will be classified for further specialized flying training leading up to appointment as a flying cadet officer for work as a pilot, navigator, or bombadier. This is from a press release, and knowing the definite preparation and careful study this fine youngster made in order that he would be selected for this training, everyone of his friends join with his parents in being very proud of the opportunity that he has for further advancement.

On Saturday mornings, we had classes that were mostly military training and at one o'clock there was a parade on the athletic field. When that was over, everybody headed for the bus waiting to take us into town. That was, everybody except those who had more than seven demerits for the week. Those unfortunate few had to stay back and walk an hour, with a wooden rifle, back and forth in front of the dorm for every demerit over seven.

I got four demerits the whole time I was at Morehead, and I got them all in one day. That particular day, it was my responsibility to make sure everybody in my room cleaned the latrine. After we cleaned it, somebody went in and washed their hands and left four drops of water in the basin. So, I got a demerit for each drop of water. The incident didn't keep me from going into town that Saturday, but it sure did aggravate me.

There wasn't that much to do in town, but it sure made for a nice change. The local folks were real nice and friendly to the soldiers. I mostly went to movies and walked around town. The bus stopped at Foss's Drug Store, so I spent a lot of time hanging out at the soda counter there. I would escape the cold by sitting at the counter drinking hot chocolate with marshmallows on top and watching the girls come and go. I exchanged smiles with a few and even talked to one or two. It was amazing what a uniform could do for a guy's confidence.

One good-looking, red-head was particularly friendly; she often came in and sat and talked to me. Her name was Lucille but everybody called her Cille. We dated for a while, but it soon became clear that she was too wild for me. She liked to party and could dance up a storm, especially the jitterbug. Guess I was just an old stick in the mud, but I didn't like to dance and I never did like a loud, crowded party either - still don't. Much to her surprise, I broke it off with her.

Then there was Norma. She was just the opposite of Cille. I met her through a friend of mine from Jacksonville. He was married, so his wife was there staying in the same boarding house as Norma. They decided to fix us up, so we all went out

together. Norma was studying to be a teacher and was wholesome and all American; I really liked her. We dated most of my time at Morehead, and I thought we might end up together. She saw me off at midnight when my train left for California. We wrote for a short time, but you know how that goes. After the war, I did think about trying to contact her, but it had been too long. I figured she was probably settled down and married by now - she was like that.

On occasion, a group of us would cross the Red River into Fargo, North Dakota, and pay a visit to the American Legion. There, when you rang the door bell somebody looked out a little sliding peep hole. Soldiers in uniform were always welcomed. It was a nice place to drink because nobody bothered you. Sometimes we would gather in a local lounge or at a house party. It was fun to watch everybody dance, especially Cille.

Singing was always a big part of training because we sang whenever we marched. Some of the words were pretty questionable, but that was all part of it. I particularly remember one about the Souse family which ticked off some guys because the language bordered on obscene. All of us southern boys got a kick out of singing *Dixie*. On occasion, at night we would all meet up in a conference room at the end of one of the halls, open all the windows, and belt out our homeland song - it ruffled a few feathers.

There was one fella who used to come in on the weekends after a night of drinking and insist that we all stay up and keep the party going. We were all ready to hit the sack and wanted no part of his foolishness, but he persisted. We got pretty tired of his shenanigans and decided to do something about it. The next time he pulled that stunt, we threw his mattress out the window and into the snow. That seemed to sober him up real fast. After that, whenever we came in from a night on the town, he was the first one in the sack.

I did well in all my class work and physical training, and I even did pretty well with the girls. The only area I didn't do well in was my ten hours of initial-flight training. The old say-

ing about crawling before walking was so true. We certainly started out crawling in 65 horse power Piper Cubs; not exactly what I had envisioned for my first flying experience. Unfortunately, my instructor was an old sorehead who was such a jerk the other instructors didn't even associate with him.

At first, I really enjoyed myself and found flying to be an exciting experience. All was well until we had to learn how to do stalls and spins. The old sore head would tell me to put it in a spin and pull it out on two and a half turns. Well, you had to count the times the earth rotates. I couldn't seem to keep up with the rotations, so I didn't fare very well in pulling the plane out of a spin on a point. Besides all that, I was never convinced that a Cub J3 was built to do spins. Guess my opinion showed because the instructor barked at me, "Your problem is you don't have any confidence in the plane." He was right on that.

My flight training continued to go downhill from there. I was about to take my first flight with me at the controls while practicing takeoffs and landings. The instructor would be up there with me, but I would handle the controls. There were snow banks piled up on each side of the taxi ways, and the wind was really whipping around the hanger. He decided that he needed to taxi it out and get the plane in position on the runway. As he was taxiing out, he caught a gust of wind, and it blew us into a snow bank and killed the engine. Well, naturally, he was real aggravated and screamed at me to get out and get it turned around till the prop was clear. As I was climbing back into the plane I made one of the biggest mistakes of my military career - I laughed.

Cadet training at Morehead State Teachers College, Minnesota

As expected, after that I could do no right. I did manage to take off just fine and flew around exactly as instructed. On the final landing, just as I was about to set her down on three points, a gust of wind hit and lifted us up. I gave it a little bit more power and instead of making a three-point landing, I just eased her down and touched the front wheels, followed by the tail wheels, and made a perfectly smooth landing. The old sorehead immediately jumped all over me. "This isn't a P-51 and you're not a GD fighter pilot!"

Keep in mind that those ten hours were just the preliminary of many more hours of flight training to become a pilot. My bad start probably would not have prevented me from becoming a pilot; what did, were orders from high above.

Chapter 9

Santa Ana Army Air Field
California
Classification

In March of '44, I was again on a troop train headed to Santa Ana, California. It was springtime in the San Fernando Valley, and the weather was absolutely beautiful. Shortly after arriving, we were standing in formation while being briefed by a student wing commander. He gave us the ins and outs of what to expect, then concluded by pointing to a snowcapped mountain off in the distance. "See that white stuff on top of that mountain? That's chicken shit and every night it slides down the mountain and covers this base."

At Santa Anna we were to be classified to determine whether we would go on to school to become a pilot, bombardier, or a navigator. Initially, our time was spent with more testing and one-on-one interviews with the training officers, doctors and psychologists.

We had been there less than two weeks when everyone in my squadron received a letter from General Hap Arnold, Commanding General of the Army Air Corp. That memo would forever change our military dreams. It read something like this:

AT THIS TIME THERE ARE TOO MANY PERSONNEL IN AIR-CREW TRAINING. YOUR SQUADRON WILL BE TAKEN OUT OF TRAINING. YOU WILL BE GIVEN YOUR CHOICE OF OTHER FIELDS THAT ARE EXPERIENCING SHORTFALLS.

A few of the guys looked like they could have cried, especially those who had college degrees because that order probably ended their chance of serving as officers. You can bet, I didn't cry; in fact, I was kind of relieved because I was so tired of going to school. I wanted to see action, not classrooms. Our field choices were airplane mechanics, radio operator, and armament. I wanted the shortest school and that turned out to be armament.

We had our bags packed and were to leave at 15:00 hours for Denver, Colorado, for 18 weeks. At 13:00 hours formation, the commanding officer made an announcement that volunteers were needed to go to gunnery school in Kingman, Arizona. He informed us that the school was only eight weeks, and when finished you would be promoted to the rank of corporal. Eight weeks sure sounded better than 18, and skipping from private to corporal was certainly appealing. I actually talked some of my buddies into going with me; it sounded like a real deal at the time.

Chapter 10

Kingman Army Air Field
Arizona
Gunnery School

By now train rides weren't so exciting. It was late March of '44 and I was headed for Kingman, Arizona. The location was in the desert, so it was hot and dry and very dusty. It was also in the middle of nowhere which really didn't matter because we weren't allowed to leave the base anyway. Early on we were warned not to even think about going AWOL.

"The mountains are further away than they look," we were told. One young soldier's story of an attempted escape went something like this: "The poor guy walked for two days. We kept watch with binoculars. By the third day he was looking pretty rough so we sent a jeep out to get him. After he got out of the hospital, he went straight to the stockade."

The school actually wasn't too bad. I began to feel like I was finally getting ready for some real action. In the classroom we practiced aircraft recognition. We also practiced taking apart and putting together .50 caliber machine guns. Eventually, we had to be able to do it blindfolded. There was a mock up of a B-17 top and ball turret which we all had to learn to operate.

We spent most of our time on the gunnery range firing the .50 calibers. There was also a skeet range where we shot twelve-gauge shotguns to get used to shooting at moving targets. They had rigged up the back of a pick-up truck with rails around the sides. We stood up and shot at the clay pigeons as the truck traveled at about 20 miles an hour around an oval track. It might sound boring, but not to me; I got to be a pretty good shot.

Finally, we were ready to go up in a real B-17. Of course, she was stripped down and in pretty rough shape, but the sound of those engines was something. I was overwhelmed by the power she possessed. I was also overwhelmed by the smell. Something about the intense heat reflecting off the runway caused the aluminum skin to kind of sweat off a terrible odor inside the plane. It went away as soon as you got some altitude and she cooled down. That smell caused lots of guys to get sick. I threw up the first time, but after that, I was okay.

In the air, we took turns firing from a waist window of the stripped down Fortress. We fired at a target that was being towed by a T-6 trainer. The target was a banner about five feet high and 30 feet long. Before we headed out, we were told to pay close attention to what was left of a crashed T-6. It seemed that one of the practicing gunners in a previous class accidentally shot the tow plane. The pilot managed to bail out safely and later found the young gunner who shot him down.

Our ammo tips were different colors because they had been dipped into colored wax. We were told that the instructors checked our accuracy, but we never got any scores or feedback. Either we all did alright, or nobody bothered to check. I think, like us, the instructors questioned if it was even necessary for us to be practicing air-to-ground firing. The whole time I was flying combat, I never knew of a gunner firing at a ground target.

One gunnery class at the time went out to an auxiliary field in the old gun town of Yucca for a week to practice firing air-to-ground. Yucca was several miles from Kingman and wasn't much more than an air strip with a few barracks. There was a mess hall and a much appreciated swimming pool. There, we shot up a lot of cactus as well as some canvas ground targets.

It was unbearably hot, so we only practiced in the early mornings and late afternoons. In the middle of the day, everybody just tried to avoid the sun and heat. The barracks at Yucca sat up about three feet off the ground, so we would crawl up under them and try to catch a nap or read and write letters. It was even too hot to get in the pool.

UNITED STATES
ARMY AIR FORCES

FLEXIBLE GUNNERY SCHOOL

Be it known that Pvt. 1cl Kenneth S. Tucker
of the United States Army Air Forces, has satisfactorily completed the course of instruction prescribed for Flexible Gunnery Training.

In testimony whereof and by virtue of vested authority I do confer upon him this

Diploma

Given at KINGMAN ARMY AIR FIELD
on this, the FOURTH *day of* JUNE *in the year of our Lord one thousand nine hundred and forty-four.*

Henry A. Detering
HENRY A. DETERING, 1st Lt., A.C.
Commanding
FOURTH STUDENT SQUADRON

Attest:

Joseph O. Freeze
JOSEPH O. FREEZE,
2nd Lt., A.C.
Ass't. Secretary.

The dust at Yucca was something awful. When we woke up, the first thing we did was gently gather the corners of our blanket and take it outside and shake out the nightly accumulation of dust. It seemed to creep into every crack and corner of the barracks. I remember dust getting up my nose, and in my eyes, mouth and hair. On the ride back to Kingman in the back of a six-by truck, it was so dusty we had to put our gas masks on to be able to breathe.

The entire time we were at Kingman, the food was terrible and everybody lost lots of weight. Daily, we were served the most awful tasting mutton stew which smelled as bad as it tasted. To this day, the smell of mutton and cooking crabs makes me gag. Later, we heard rumors that the base supply officer and the mess officer were selling our government rations on the black market and buying cheap mutton from the local ranchers - I hope they were hanged.

It was at Kingman where I celebrated my 19th birthday. I don't remember any partying, but I do remember mail call. The mail clerk handed me a handful of mail, obviously cards. He looked up at me, grinned, and said, "Happy Birthday!"

After finishing gunnery school in June of '44, we were awarded our wings, but instead of being promoted to corporal, as promised, we were promoted to private first class. What could we do except chalk it up to a typical war time SNAFU? We were just glad to get out of there.

Chapter 11

Lincoln Army Air Field
Nebraska
Staging

Next stop...Lincoln, Nebraska, which was a staging area for further reassignments. Because Lincoln was a staging area, there was no training. We just pulled details like mowing grass or any menial jobs around the base. Seems I always got stuck painting; never did like to paint and I still don't. Since we weren't training, everything was real relaxed. We just lined up in formation every morning; the duty officer would count off a certain number of us to go mow, or a certain number to go paint, etc. He would hand one of us a clipboard with the assignment, and off we'd go.

It didn't take me long to figure out that there had to be a way around all that foolishness. I bided my time for a day or two and carefully observed the procedure. On a previous detail, I spied a handsaw that had been left behind, so I casually picked it up and carried it back to the barracks with me. After discovering the saw, when I reported for formation, I would head toward the back. Up front, when the duty officer started counting off guys for details, I'd head out, carrying that saw, like I was on a mission. Nobody ever questioned me, and I didn't even have a clipboard. I would head directly to the library and hide the saw behind the door. There, I would spend the day searching the shelves for anything that interested me. The chairs were comfortable and the bathrooms were clean.

The plan worked beautifully for a few days until somebody stole my saw.

Fortunately, I had a couple of real smart buddies who came up with a simple, but ingenious way to also get us out of details. Because the duty officer started in the front forming his crews, we lined up in back. One of my buddies had gotten a hold of a clipboard, and while the duty officer was busy up front, he would count us off and march us down the sidewalk like we were on a mission. Our hideout was among shrubs on the back side of a hill not far from the mess hall. We had to be quiet, so mostly we snoozed and read - nobody ever missed us.

Several times a week, a few buddies and myself would venture into Lincoln and make the rounds of the local watering holes. We soon learned that there was a city ordinance which required drinkers to be seated at all times. In other words, you couldn't go up to the bar, buy a drink, and carry it back to a table. You either had to sit at the bar and drink or sit at a table and be waited on. As strange as it was, the ordinance was strictly enforced.

One night, three of us left a bar and were walking down the street when one of the guys pulled out a half pint from his back pocket and took a swig. A military police officer pulled up, got out, confiscated the bottle and told us all to get in the car. He took us to an MP station in town where a sergeant informed us that we had violated the town's drinking ordinance. The sergeant let us go, but he wouldn't let my buddy have his bottle back.

After several days of that nonsense, we were given a ten day leave to go home for the last time. I remember catching a train to Atlanta and then a bus to Apalachicola. After travel time, I would only have three days at home. Those three days were spent pretty close to home; I just wanted to be with my family.

One of those precious days I spent with my brother. We took off one day, just the two of us, in Arthur's 1936 Ford sedan and drove west along the coast until we reached Panama City. Back in those days that was a good distance for a day trip.

We stopped at the Tally-Ho Drive-In for lunch and got a big kick out of the car hops. Our girl was real cute and friendly, and she came back to check on us numerous times. It soon became pretty obvious that she was flirting with my brother even though his crutches were laying in plain view on the back seat. I teased him unmercifully about her the rest of my time at home. He later wrote that he made a few trips back to the Tally-Ho, but the relationship never got past the tray attached to his rolled-down window. The Tally-Ho is still there today and they still have car hops.

Before heading home, we had a "cool one" in a little bar near the city marina. I'll never forget having that day to share with my big brother. Like Dad and me, he kept up with the war efforts. He gave me lots of advice, just like an older brother should, and reminded me that I would be fighting for both of us.

As expected, the goodbyes were sad for all of us, but my family knew how excited I was and how anxious I was to get on my way. They were all so brave and proud at that final goodbye. I later learned that as soon as my bus pulled off, my dad had a heart attack. He spent several days in bed but did recover. The stress of knowing what I was about to face was just too much for him.

Chapter 12

Alexandria Army Air Field
Louisiana
Air Crew Training

Shortly after returning to Lincoln, I was aboard another troop train headed to Alexandria Army Air Field, Louisiana, for Air-Crew Training. Upon arriving, I found that I had already been assigned to a crew. I knew that my crew, especially the pilot, was going to play a huge role in my survival. I'm not sure how the crews were formed; maybe the pilots got to pick or maybe the group operations officer did the crewing up. Regardless, I found my name listed under crew 7252.

As I settled into my barracks, the sound of my name being called startled me, "Tucker!" When I reported to the opened door, there stood a small group of soldiers. They were all smiling and seemed to be in pretty good spirits. The obvious leader of the group stepped forward, shook my hand and said, "Hello Private Tucker, I'm Lieutenant Dunigan, pilot of crew 7252. I'm happy to meet you and glad to welcome you to the crew."

I immediately had a good feeling about that group. They had all just met but already seemed relaxed and comfortable with each other. After Dunigan introduced himself the others did the same. After their name, each one told where they were from. Everybody had to add, for various reasons, why their home town or home state was about the best place on earth. It seemed that when you were a long way from home and in a strange environment, home suddenly became a very special place.

When we dispersed, I remember feeling a huge sense of belonging. I felt so confident that the ten of us were going to come together as a strong and supportive team. I was anxious to get started with our training and see just what we could do as a crew.

Our ground-school training consisted mostly of aircraft recognition and crew procedures. Thankfully, that went by quickly and we were soon ready for in-flight training. Before we got started, Lt. Dunigan assembled the four gunners and told us to decide which positions we wanted. His only suggestion was that since Jack Taylor was the shortest, he should take the ball turret. Michael Joyce quickly spoke up, "Sir, I request one of the waist windows. I get claustrophobic in cramped spaces, and the tail looks pretty tight to me." That left Kenneth Snow and me; neither of us had a preference, but finally he said he would take a waist window. I was fine with the tail.

Our pilot was 1st Lieutenant Louis J. Dunigan from Casper, Wyoming, and a graduate of the University of Wyoming.

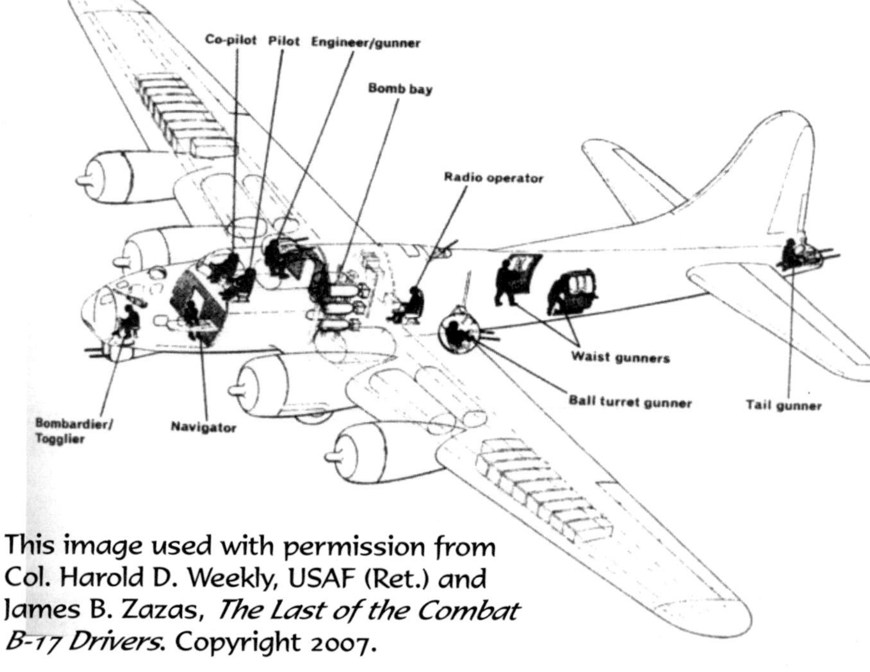

This image used with permission from Col. Harold D. Weekly, USAF (Ret.) and James B. Zazas, *The Last of the Combat B-17 Drivers*. Copyright 2007.

He proudly wore one of the few "I Saw It Coming" ribbons - meaning he enlisted in the military before Pearl Harbor. At that time he had been in the Army but decided he wanted to fly, so he transferred into the Army Air Corp. He started out training to be a fighter pilot in the P-47s, but the rapid changes in altitude caused him to have sinus problems. Lucky for us, he transferred into multi-engine aircraft training.

We considered him an "old man" because he was 27 years old and married. He was a Christian and didn't drink, smoke, or use profanity. Next to my father, there has never been another man I respected and admired more than Louis Dunigan.

Dunigan was a natural leader; his responsibility as the aircraft commander was never questioned. As first pilot, he was always in control of the aircraft during the most difficult situations such as take-offs, formations and landings. It was obvious that his first concern was always the well-being of his crew, in the air and on the ground.

Our co-pilot was 2nd Lt. James W. Garrison from Norfolk, Virginia. He was a really nice guy who, like Dunigan, was a Christian and didn't smoke, drink or use profanity. He was engaged to a girl whose last name was Harrison, so he joked that he was going to change her H to a G. To break the monotony on missions, Garrison became our punster. He would get on the intercom and spring a pun on us. Everybody would groan, but we were always curious to see what he would come up with. It's funny, but I can't remember a single one of Garrison's puns.

Garrison was second in command and was responsible for knowing the duties of every member of the crew. It was his responsibility to see that all members of the crew were working together as a team. He had to be thoroughly familiar with the operations of the aircraft in case anything happened to the pilot. When conditions weren't so hazardous, the co-pilot would take over the controls. Garrison was a good pilot, but I always felt safer with Dunigan at the helm.

Second Lt. Halsey S. Nisula was our navigator. He was from Gardener, Massachusetts, and another nice guy. I liked

him immediately because he was quiet, like me. He was 23 and had worked at an A&P grocery store before enlisting.

The navigator's job was to keep us on course and get us to the target and back. At all times, he had to know the exact location of the plane; he seemed to have maps everywhere. Another one of his responsibilities was to call for a crew oxygen check every ten minutes when we were at high altitudes. He also was responsible for keeping a very detailed flight log. If we spotted anything out of the ordinary we would call the navigator and give him a report. The success of a mission greatly depended on the skills of the pilot and navigator and their ability to work together.

FO/Donald H. McQuistion was our bombardier. Everybody called him Mac. He was a flight officer which was the equivalent of today's warrant officer. The best I remember, he was from New Jersey and attended Rutgers. It was the bombardier's job to set up the Norden bombsight so when we reached the target he would be prepared to drop the bombs. The Norden was a complicated instrument that was connected to the controls of the bomber. The Norden bombsight was considered top secret, so the navigator was responsible for destroying it if the plane went down. If we were in a G model there would be two .50 caliber machine guns mounted in a chin turret under the Plexiglas nose of the plane. It was also the bombardier's job to man those guns.

When we got overseas there was a shortage of bombardiers, which caused McQuistion to be in great demand. To make up for the shortage, toggliers were often used; most of the toggliers were T/Sgt. They didn't use the bomb site; instead, they watched the lead plane and dropped their bombs when the bombardier in the lead plane did.

T/Sgt. Clyde Dwight Jr. was the flight engineer and top-turret gunner. He was a six-foot Texan and another of the "old men" also at 27. He was married and had a daughter. Before enlisting, he had worked in the oil fields in and around his home town of Pampa, Texas. First and foremost, he was an aircraft mechanic, but he was also trained as a gunner.

During flight, Dwight stood between the pilot and co-pilot and kept an eye on the instruments. It was his job to know the mechanics of every operating part of the airplane. If anything went wrong, he had to know how to fix it. When we were in enemy territory, or if German fighters were spotted, he stood up in the top turret and manned two .50 caliber machine guns.

The radio operator, Buck/Sgt. Malcom Vignes, was from Louisiana. He said he wasn't a Cajun, but he sure sounded like one. He claimed his mother was Huey P. Long's secretary when he was assassinated.

Vignes had his own little radio room with a small table and chair. His compartment held receivers, transmitters, and other communication equipment which he used to maintain and monitor incoming and outgoing messages. He kept in contact with ground stations and kept us updated with position reports. There was a single .50 caliber machine gun mounted in a dome in the top of the radio room.

Our right-waist gunner was Corporal Michael E. Joyce from Holyoke, Massachusetts, an Irishman and another "old man" of 27. He was married and had a small son. He was a nice guy but kind of ornery sometimes. When he came in at night from the club or a mission, he would wake everybody up. No matter how much we complained, he just didn't care. Guess he figured if he was up, everybody needed to be up.

At left waist was PFC (private first class) Kenneth Snow from Oklahoma. His father was a captain in the Army. We were the same age, 18, and seemed to have a lot in common. He was a real nice guy, and we quickly became good friends.

The waist gunner's job was to ward off any attacking enemy fighters that came into sight from their side of the plane. They stood in front of the waist window and manned a single Browning .50 caliber machine gun.

PFC Jack R.Taylor from Beaumont, Texas, was the ball-turret gunner. He was also 18 and was kind of a spoiled, only child. Everybody thought he was the youngest of the crew when actually I was. His duty was to protect the vulnerable underbelly of the plane. To do that, he climbed into the electrically powered turret during a mission and manned two .50 caliber machine guns. He was isolated from the rest of the crew and had to perform his duties in very close, cramped quarters.

Then there was me, PFC Kenneth S. Tucker, tail gunner. To reach my position I had to crawl through a tunnel-like opening in the rear of the plane and then ease myself down into a sitting position onto a bicycle seat. Conditions were very cramped with very little room to move my legs. In rough air, tail gunners had to have a strong resistance to airsickness. I maneuvered two .50 caliber machine guns as I constantly scanned my 180 degree view of hostile skies. I, too, was completely isolated back there; the only way I could communicate was through the plane's intercom system.

People have often told me I was crazy for taking the tail when I didn't have to. The choice seemed to suit me, maybe because I was always pretty much a loner. I knew I would be more comfortable back there than some others.

Part of our training took place on some cross-country trips which were mainly for the pilot and navigator to practice coordinating, but we all went along for the ride. One flight took us to Arizona and over the Grand Canyon where Dunigan took her down below the realm. We had about a mile or so clearance on each side so it wasn't a dare-devil stunt or anything like that; it was just a spectacular sight-seeing trip.

On some of our practice runs, we flew over to a bombing range in Orange, Texas, near the Gulf Coast. Our practice bombs were called "blue birds." They weren't loaded with explosives, just black powder to mark hits. One time, during our take-off roll, our hydraulic system went out. Dunigan cut the engines and quickly veered right to get off the runway and out of the way of oncoming planes. We ended up in some high weeds. As we were getting out, Jack and I thought our situation was amusing and were having a laugh. Well, Dunigan wasn't amused in the least and gave us a lecture on the seriousness of the situation and informed us that it was no laughing matter - we got the message.

Standing L to R: Clyde Dwight, Malcom Vignes, Michael Joyce, Jack Taylor, Kenneth Snow and Kenneth Tucker. Squatting L to R: Louis Dunigan, James Garrsion, Halsey Nisula and Donald McQuistion

We had another mishap involving those blue-bird bombs. After the mission, McQuistion discovered that one of the bombs had gotten hung up, so Dunigan told him to drop it into one of the many swamp areas we flew over on the way back to base. Well, somebody saw us drop the bomb and reported the mishap. I'm not sure who received the report, but we were soon joined by two P-47s from Barksdale Army Air Field near Shreveport. They came to check us out and escorted us all the way back to our base.

On our training runs, Dunigan always found something for the gunners to do. He required us to stay awake and alert at all times. One practice he had us do was to come up to the flight deck, one at a time, to get the feel of the aircraft. Dunigan would put the aircraft on automatic pilot and have us sit in the pilot seat. Garrison would be the instructor and teach us how to guide the planc.

Everyone enjoyed the experience except Michael Joyce, the right-waist gunner. He was the one who refused to get in the tail or the ball turret; he wouldn't have gone back in the tail under the threat of death. He also wanted no part of going into the flight deck. Dunigan tried to talk him into it and ultimately could have ordered him to. Instead, Dunigan let it go and didn't make a big deal about it.

I was more than happy to take a turn in the pilot seat any time Dunigan offered. I was amazed at just how sluggish and slow those big bombers were. Garrison was a great instructor and taught me a lot. The hardest thing for me to do was keep the altitude constant. I kept looking at the rate-of-climb indicator and Garrison would say, "Don't look at that. It's too sensitive." To prove his point, he took out a handkerchief and hung it on a knob to cover up the indicator. He told me to just watch the artificial horizon, which I did. In a minute or two I had her going straight and level.

Dunigan's reason for wanting us to get the feel of the plane was because of an incident he read about that happened early in the war in the Eighth Air Force out of England. In that particular event, the pilot and co-pilot had been hit. One of the gunners was able to take over the controls and bring the plane home. Because of his actions, the gunner received the Congressional Medal of Honor for saving the lives of the crew. Fortunately, he had been a washed out cadet, so he did have quite a few hours in the air. Thank goodness for me and the rest of the crew, nobody other than the pilot or co-pilot ever had to try to bring us home.

Toward the end of our training, we would rotate between day time training and night flying. The night flights were mostly for navigation exercises. That's when we found out that Nisula was the best navigator we could have possible hoped for. One time we were flying a round robin to St. Louis and Dallas and back. When we arrived in St. Louis, we kidded him about being twenty seconds off in his calculation.

It soon became apparent that Dunigan was an outstanding pilot; he was calm and confident. I'm so thankful that my pilot was an old experienced man of 27 and not some hot-shot

20-year-old kid. I had a good feeling about him right away. I knew if anybody could take us there and back it would be Dunigan.

I was impressed beyond belief at how well our crew worked together as a team. When we were in the air, each member showed unbelievable skill and dedication to the crew. The same was true on the ground; we looked out for each other. There was no doubt in my mind that we were an awesome crew, and it soon became apparent that those guys were now part of my extended family.

There must have been 50 or 60 crews in our training cycle. Out of all those crews, we managed to win the Most Outstanding Crew Award. Well, that was certainly no surprise to me. Obviously, the instructors saw what I had already observed. Our award was all the money left over in the squadron fund. Dunigan wouldn't let the officers have their share. True to his character, he made sure the money was divided evenly between the six enlisted men. I think we ended up with about nine dollars each - which we immediately blew.

After completing crew training and preparing to leave for overseas, we received a disturbing order that one of the gunners had to be left behind. The reason, we were told, was that there were extra gunners overseas because when planes were shot up or lost, some of the crew survived. There were gunners over there with no crew, so we would have to pick up one of those displaced gunners.

When Dunigan asked the four of us for a volunteer, nobody would. In that case, the wing commander had ordered that it had to be the left-waist gunner; that was Kenneth Snow. I sure hated to see him go because we had become good friends. He took the news better than I did - I never saw him again.

When we weren't training, we spent time at the base swimming pool, service club and library. I especially enjoyed the library because I had access to books on just about any subject imaginable. The enlisted guys on the crew all stuck close together. We seemed to always be doing something, and I don't ever remember being bored or lonely.

Before long, we noticed that a lot of the crews were wearing matching baseball caps. It was a nice gesture and made some of the crews really stand out. Everyone on my crew liked the idea of getting matching caps and decided to do one better and grow matching mustaches. Michael already had a full mustache which motivated the rest of us to catch up to him. That was, everybody except Dwight, our flight engineer. He complained, "I'll be damned if I'm going to cultivate something under my nose that grows wild around my ass." He didn't like it, but he folded to peer pressure and gave in. We all looked darn good. Dunigan kept his mustache the whole time we were overseas.

I have some real fond memories of the town of Alexandria, Louisiana. A buddy suggested we go to the Hotel Bentley; he had heard that they had good music. Imagine our delight when we entered The Mirror Room and discovered a string quartet made up of four young women. We managed to get a front row table and, sure enough, during the first intermission we all started talking. They were all real friendly and as pretty as their music.

We soon learned that the two violin players and the cello player were from The Philharmonic Orchestra of Kansas City, and the piano player was a professional musician who had joined up with the others. One of the violin players caught my fancy. Her name was Lucille (yes, another Lucille). I quickly became a regular and sat at a front row table whenever I could get away from the base. She liked me because I appreciated her music; so whenever I came in, she made sure the group played all my favorite songs.

Sometimes, during intermission, Lucille and I would walk down the street to a little sandwich shop. At first it made me real uncomfortable because everybody stared at us. Of course they stared. Guess it would have been kind of strange to be sitting in a sandwich shop and see a beautiful woman all dressed up in a full length evening gown come strolling in for a snack.

Other times, we went up to the girls' suite during intermission. One night, shortly before we left for overseas, I was surprised to notice one of our parachute covers thrown carelessly in a corner. Imagine my surprise when, upon further investigation, I saw the stenciled T2107 which identified it as my missing parachute. I had reported mine missing just a few days earlier and had no idea how it ended up in a suite at the Bentley Hotel.

The girls knew I was mad, so they quickly began to explain that a guy who was sweet on the other violin player had given it to them; he told them it was surplus. They were thrilled because they could use the parachute to make slips and pajamas or whatever. I was anything but thrilled and was glad the guy wasn't there because that gave me some time to think about what I wanted to do.

My first thought was to turn him in, but then I decided, no, that would delay him going overseas with the rest of us. We were all leaving in a few days, and I wanted him to be with us. That way, he wouldn't miss a single opportunity to be cannon fodder.

Just before we shipped out, Charlotte, the cello player, announced she was going to marry a 2nd Lt. she had been dating. A lot of that went on during war time, but it sure seemed like a dumb thing to do. I couldn't understand how a man, who was about to go into combat, could ask a woman to make a lifetime commitment when he could not count on a future at all. Who knows? Maybe they lived happily ever after.

Lucille and I said our good-byes. We wrote for awhile but, she moved on with the quartet, and we soon lost touch.

Chapter 13

The Trip Over

The squadron left Alexandria on October 10, 1944, and took a train back to Lincoln, Nebraska, where we checked out a brand new B-17G fresh from the factory. We took two test flights there at Lincoln and were impressed with our first experience in a G model. I was especially impressed with the increased size of the tail compartment. There was twice as much room and also more Plexiglas, so the visibility was much better; I joked about my greenhouse.

From Lincoln, we were to proceed to Grinier Field, New Hampshire, right outside Manchester, and wait for further orders. We refueled and spent one night. The Red Cross gave everybody a little bag with toilet articles. To my surprise and delight they also gave each crew a football. Everyplace we stopped after that, we threw that football around.

Our orders were to proceed to Gander Lake, Newfoundland, with the code name, Bayline Fox. When we took off from Grinier, we didn't fly in formation. Instead, our instructions were to take off separately with a lone aircraft taking off every few minutes. Dunigan had a great idea, "Well, we're going to be passing close by Niagara Falls so we may as well take a detour and have a look." So we turned off course and soon saw two other planes way up ahead of us; everybody was doing the same thing. We got a big bird's eye view of Niagara Falls, and it was something to see.

We ended up staying at Gander Lake for three or four nights because a weather front in the Atlantic kept us grounded.

We had to have clear weather at night because the navigator had to see the stars. At that time, there were no radio beams that would reach out to the middle of the Atlantic Ocean.

Gander Lake was a pretty desolate place, so there was very little to do. The football helped pass the time, and we even went canoeing. One night, there was a beautiful full moon, so after supper we all went for a moon-light stroll down by the lake. We ran into another B-17 crew and Dunigan started talking to their pilot. They were doing the same thing, just killing time. For lack of anything better to do, the two pilots decided that we needed to have a sing along. So there we were, two B-17 crews, down by the lake, in the moonlight, having a sing along. Dunigan lead us in some of our old basic-training songs. We actually sounded pretty good - it was a great time.

Finally, we left Gander Lake with a compass heading and instructions to open our sealed orders two hours after take-off. Some pilots probably opened their orders as soon as they were off the ground, but not Dunigan. After two hours we learned that, after several stops, our final destination was Gioia, Italy.

So now we knew that we were not going to be joining the illustrious 8th Air Force in England. We were not going to be in an English-speaking country with friendly neighbors and pretty local girls to date. We wouldn't have local pubs to visit or weekend passes to London. There was little chance that Andy Rooney or Walter Cronkite would be paying us a visit. The war correspondents wanted assignments where they had access to comfortable hotels and good meals. No chance that Major Clark Gable would grace us with an appearance. He was a glamour boy who had been assigned to the 8th to help boost their glamorous reputation. Bob Hope's USO Shows probably wouldn't make it to our area either. No, we were headed to the not-so-glamorous, 15th Air Force.

Our next stop was Lajes Field in the Azores, where we were supposed to spend the night in the transient barracks. When we got there, it was ratty and full of some kind of biting insects, and it stunk. It was so uninviting we decided to go sleep in the airplane. Our down-filled sleeping bags kept us warm as we stretched out all over our plane and slept that night. When we stepped out the next morning there was an odor just like we had smelled the day before. That whole place stunk; we sure were glad to get out of that rat hole.

Next stop was Marrakesh, Morocco, where we stayed for two nights. The accommodations must have been better because I don't remember sleeping in the plane again. Just at sun up one morning, several of us were out walking around, just killing time before breakfast. We happened upon an old abandoned mosque and climbed up to the top to have a look out across the desert. Out in the distance was an amazing sight - a camel caravan headed into town from the desert. For a moment I felt like Lawrence of Arabia. Now, that was a sight to see, and probably for the first time, I began to realize that I really was a very long way from home.

On our way down from the mosque, we had our first encounter with Kilroy. Whoever he was, he had been there before and had left graffiti on the wall to prove it. There were lots of tales about how the craze got started, but the one I think is most likely is that it originated with a guy named Kilroy who inspected troopships. As troops boarded, they noticed the strange markings left by Kilroy to prove that he had, indeed, been there before them as an inspector. Evidently, some of the troops took a liking to the little man peeking over a wall with just his eyes and nose showing. It got to be a challenge to be the first to put the Kilroy graffiti in every place imaginable throughout Europe and the South Pacific.

The next afternoon, some of the other enlisted guys and myself were walking around the outskirts of the base when we came upon a compound surrounded by about a ten-foot rock wall; turned out, it was an Italian war prison. What was so memorable about the place was that some of the prisoners were perched high up in trees, just up over the top of the wall. One guy began to yell at us and gestured for us to come closer. When we were close enough, he threw an object over the wall and gestured for us to pick it up and have a look. The object turned out to be a cigarette lighter. Somehow, the prisoners were making lighters out of aluminum, probably from crashed airplanes and were trying to sell them to the American soldiers who walked by. Someone in the group indicated that he wanted to buy one, so the prisoner threw a little wooden box over the wall for the interested party to put the money in and throw back. That had to be one of the strangest transactions I've ever witnessed.

Our stroll continued on around to the front gate of the compound where we encountered a Moorish prison guard. He was a classic with his red fez lampshade looking hat. We asked him where we could get some vino. He leaned his rifle up against the wall, gestured for us to wait there, and took off around the wall. In no time, he was back with a quart of wine. Guess guarding the prison wasn't his top priority that day.

I enjoyed the flight to Tunis, Tunisia, because it was a low level, daytime flight. The scenery was beautiful because we flew along the side of the Atlas Mountains. We only spent one

night in Tunis which happened to be movie night. There was an outdoor theater set up right under the flight pattern. I have no memory of the movie, probably because I didn't hear half of what was said.

We took off from Tunis the next morning and headed out over the edge of the Mediterranean Sea. Near the shore, the water was clear enough to see the outline and shadows of planes that were resting on the bottom. I figured there must be plenty of downed planes all up and down the Mediterranean Coast of North Africa. I also figured there were plenty more in the deep waters that weren't visible.

Finally, we landed in Gioia in southern Italy. From there, we were loaded into the back of a big Army six-by truck and transported to Foggia and finally on to our base at Amendola where we were assigned to the 414th Bomb Squadron of the 97th Bomb Group. That's when we realized we had lost our brand new, top of the line G model aircraft. We would soon learn that it wasn't a good idea to get too attached to any one plane.

Amendola, Italy
Our New Home

Chapter 14

Getting Settled

It was dark and raining the night of November 1, 1944, when we arrived at our final destination which turned out to be the little farming village of Amendola, between Foggia and the Adriatic Sea. The truck came to a stop in front of the squadron operations building. The operations officer came out wearing full rain gear right down to some oversized galoshes. He sloshed around to the back of the truck and looked us over. It was obvious that he was not happy about the late hour or the weather conditions. We all sat there not saying a word, waiting for orders.

Then he gave me a fright when he barked, "Who's the tail gunner on this crew?"

I quickly raised my hand and answered, "I am, Sir."

He just looked at me, shook his head, turned and walked off. Dunigan quickly tried to reassure me, "Don't pay any attention to him, Tuck. That was just his lame attempt at trying to initiate us into the world of combat." Lame or not, I didn't let his actions bother me. I was confident my life was in good hands with such a great pilot and crew; besides, I was way too excited to let some old fart intimidate me.

In a few minutes, the old fart returned to inform us that he couldn't locate a tent for the enlisted men. We would have to wait until morning and take it up with the supply sergeant. The truck driver was anxious to get on his way, so we got dumped out in the pouring rain with all our gear. The five of us ended up spending our first night sleeping on the wooden tables in the mess hall. Of course, we had to get up before they served breakfast, so we rolled up our sleeping bags, gathered up our gear, and moved everything to the day room.

From there, we reported to the orderly room and found the supply sergeant who had managed to locate a tent for us. Luckily, it had stopped raining; so we picked out a spot and proceeded to put up our new home, only to discover that there were no tent poles, just the one center pole. We never did find out where Dwight got them, but he headed out through the olive grove and was gone quite awhile before he showed up with the rest of the poles. He was our flight engineer and definitely the leader of the enlisted men.

Once the tent was up, we got our cots inside and at least had a dry place to throw our duffle bags. The next order of business was to figure out a way to store our personal gear so it would stay safe and dry and out of the way. That was going to be a difficult task since the floor was one big mud puddle. Once again Dwight and a couple others went out to see what they could scrounge up. They soon returned with discarded wooden ammunition boxes which we promptly broke apart and lined the muddy floor. The boxes that were not used for the floor made pretty good makeshift foot lockers. They slid perfectly up under our cots which made it real easy to reach down, slide them out, and grab whatever you needed. The setup worked real nice when you were already laying in bed and wanted to retrieve reading or writing material.

The latrine and showers were about 100-150 yards from our tent. There were no sidewalks, just a path through the mud. The latrine was a six or eight holer set over an open pit with no partitions of any kind. It didn't just smell; it stunk. Every few days lime was thrown in the pit, but it didn't help much. And, there was no heat which made sitting there with your bare butt exposed to the elements pretty uncomfortable.

The mess hall wasn't so bad. I'll definitely have to say that we had the best cooks in the business. Our cooks did the best they could with what they had, which wasn't much.

Somehow, they managed to be creative with the rations and served up some tasty meals. Nothing was fresh; everything was either canned, dried, or powdered. Folks can joke about Spam all they want, but I'll defend the old Army staple. When fried up nice and brown and hot, Spam was quite tasty. I continued to eat Spam, in moderation, after the war, but I can't say that I've had any in the past several years. It took me a little while to get used to the powdered eggs, but before long, they tasted pretty good. On every table sat a bottle of chili sauce which we heaped on the powdered eggs to help camouflage the taste. There was always plenty of good, hot, fresh coffee; that was very important before an early morning mission. Coffee is still an important part of my early morning routine.

When you finished your meal, you took your mess kit out the backdoor and raked the scraps into a large garbage can. The knife, fork and spoon had slots; you could slide them down on the handle of your mess kit. Then you walked past two oil-fired tanks: the first held a pot of boiling, soapy water, the second held boiling, fresh water. As you walked by, you sloshed your mess kit up and down a couple of times in each tank.

After a long first day, we settled in for the first night in our tent and were happy to discover that it wasn't too bad. Thankfully, we were dry and out of the mud. As we lay in our cots that first night, Dwight was full of ideas to improve our new home. Before daybreak, we all knew the first priority would be a heater. We knew Dwight would take care of us. He had worked in the oil fields in Texas, and he seemed to know how to fix or fix up just about anything.

The next day there was an orientation briefing for the new crews. It was the usual stuff, you know, "Welcome to the 97th Bomb Group." The top brass was introduced, after which, they immediately left. Our first sergeant gave us the rundown about what we could expect as far as rules and regulations, things to do there on the base, what to do and not do in Foggia, etc.

Then an intelligence officer gave us a brief overview and advice on what to do if we survived a crash landing or a jump in enemy territory. Most of what he said I expected until he warned us about the barbaric Ustashi who could be identified by a U on their caps. If we were captured by the group, our best hope was to be turned over to the Germans. The Ustashi were known to use primitive and sadistic methods to murder Orthodox Serbs and Jews in Yugoslavia. They were to be avoided at all cost.

After the orientation, we had time to wander around and familiarize ourselves with the area. When I think back, mostly I remember tents and mud. There were no paved streets or sidewalks, just lanes that ran between the lines of tents through the mud. There was nothing scenic; even the olive groves were drab.

Squadron Operations and Orderly Room

97th Bomb Group Headquarters

There were a few permanent buildings on the base. An old, brick farmhouse had been converted into Squadron Operations with an Orderly Room on one side and Intelligence Office and Squadron Medical Facilities on the other. The squadron commander and flight surgeon lived upstairs. A huge barn had been turned into Group Headquarters. A few buildings, such as the mess halls and service clubs, had been built out of limestone for the Americans.

True to form, when we returned, Dwight had managed to scavenge materials for our much needed heater. He had discovered the airplane bone yard and no telling what other sources. Under his direction, we soon had a heating system that would help keep our tent warm during the freezing Italian winter of 1944-45. We started by building a wooden rack outside our tent to hold a 55-gallon drum of fuel oil. Then we ran a pipe under the tent floor which came up on the side of a ten-gallon oil container into which Dwight had cut a door. He had rigged up a valve that we could regulate to drip a tiny amount of fuel into a small K-ration can. He had cut a hole in the top of the container to run a stack pipe up through the top of the tent. There he attached some kind of metal dome to keep the rain and snow out.

You can imagine how dangerous those heaters were; as a precaution, we always turned ours off at night when the last person turned in. Our down-filled, mummy-type sleeping bags actually did keep us warm. I only remember one tent burning up that winter. The guys left the heater on while they were at the club and it overheated and blew up. They were lucky their only problem was looking for new quarters.

During our first few days there, we had the honor of having the officers share our latrine. It seemed that an unknown group of enlisted men had gotten teed off at some of the officers on a recent mission. To retaliate, they set the officer's latrine on fire, and it burned to the ground. The situation was really awkward for us because the only officers we recognized were the ones on our crew. For awhile there, we had to be careful what we said. We couldn't complain about how stupid a previous mission had been handled or question the intelligence of the idiot who picked the target. It was kind of tough sitting there not knowing who was taking a dump next to you. I had trouble looking at some of the officers with the same respect after I had seen them sitting on the pot with their pants down. We were all relieved when the officers' latrine was rebuilt.

Before long, our pitiful but functional wooden plank floor would be replaced with brick. Dwight had spotted a newly delivered load of bricks stacked in front of Group Headquarters. Under cover of darkness, he had us all hauling bricks back to the tent for our new and improved floor. Before long, other tent dwellers saw us and soon joined in the brick floor assembly line. That brick floor sure made our tent feel cozy and more like home.

Understandably, the next morning, some engineer was hot on the trail of the brick thieves. Of course, we were immediately discovered and at first were told we would have to return our bootie. Before that happened, Doc Remley intervened and convinced the head honchos that the brick floors needed to stay put. He argued that the morale of the enlisted men was at stake. When Doc Remley spoke, people listened. The doctor and the chaplain were definitely the two most powerful men in the squadron.

Dwight soon noticed that all the other tents had wooden doors, so nothing would do but for us to have one too. There's no telling where he got the door. He probably confiscated it right off a door frame somewhere because it came with hinges

Our home

which attached perfectly to the frame he had already built. In no time, we had a first-class door with a leather strap for a latch. Anything anybody else had, we soon had one better.

The usual water supply for the tents was several five-gallon jerry cans that were filled for us every few days. It soon became obvious that there had to be a better way to have access to our water. Once again, Dwight had a plan. He lugged in a wing tank off a P-38 which we easily strapped to some branches up in an olive tree right by our tent. Then, he ran a pipe with a shut-off valve down to a makeshift stand that he built to hold our wash basins. Our basins were actually the metal shells of our ground helmets. They made useful water basins which we used to wash up, shave, and brush our teeth. Sometimes, if it was freezing cold we'd attempt to hold the basin between our knees and sit inside by the heater.

Our first few days were spent as a crew on familiarization runs in the local area to get to know the terrain. Dunigan and Garrison needed to practice taking off and landing because soon they would be doing so in fast-paced and crowded conditions. Also, the landing strip, which was made of steel mats that had been bolted together, was not in the best condition. Our flight engineer and radio operator also needed to get acclimated and prepared for the fast pace of combat missions. The gunners all fired several practice rounds mostly aiming at shrubs and trees. When a sheep herder and his flock came into view, we ceased firing until he was out of sight. We were all too aware that we would soon be heading to much more dangerous skies.

It didn't take long for us to become very aware that Italy was in sad shape because of the war. I couldn't help but feel sorry for the Italian people. Their country had been ravaged by the Germans and Americans. Towns around rail yards and industries were especially torn up. From the air, it was obvious that the Italian people had a pretty miserable existence.

The gunners didn't need as much time on the familiarization runs as the others. We flew on two or three runs, then Dunigan told us to use the extra ground time to get to know the place and figure out what we were going to do when we weren't flying.

Chapter 15

Life on the Base

When I think back on what I did during my free time, mostly, I remember reading, writing in my diary and writing letters home. I was very fortunate to get lots of mail which was what I looked most forward to. I also enjoyed answering my mail because when I was writing home, somehow home didn't seem so far away. My dad's letters were the ones I remember the most because he was the only one who knew what it was like to fight in a war. His letters were always full of advice and encouragement and, above all, he always reminded me how proud he was.

We had to turn in our mail to Dunigan to be censored. Either he or another one of our officers had to read every letter we wrote home. The guys with wives and girlfriends didn't particularly like their commanding officers reading their love letters. The main reason for the censoring was to make sure no information leaked out that might be of benefit to the enemy. I think, probably too, it was a way for our commanding officers to check on our morale and emotional well being.

For writing letters home, we used a one-page form called V-mail. After passing censorship, the page was microfilmed then sent to the States. Upon arrival, our one-page letters were developed and sent on to their destination. Not exactly high tech, but the process did speed things up a little.

Special Services had all kinds of football and baseball equipment. There were even a couple sets of horseshoes which I enjoyed because I had never played before. When the weather was good I enjoyed tossing around a football and playing in a touch game every now and then. Sometimes there would be 15 guys on one team. It didn't matter, we were just trying to get some exercise and have a little fun. All was well until some ex-pro quarterback showed up and caused everybody to argue over which team he would be on.

Mostly ground crew played on the organized teams. Guys on flight crews weren't allowed to play on the teams because we couldn't risk getting hurt and not being able to fly. The safety of our hands was the biggest concern. If we broke or bruised our hands then we wouldn't be able to get those thick gloves on which we had to wear to keep from getting frostbite. With an injured hand, a gunner certainly couldn't fire his guns properly.

In the spring, the squadron started up an organized baseball team. There were some really good players, and the manager had played AAA baseball. I often went out and watched them practice and got to be friends with the manager. When there was a home game and I wasn't flying, I'd go out and cheer them on. I even traveled to a couple of away games and particularly remember one team was an all black service unit. I got the biggest kick out of watching those guys play. They had some pretty unorthodox moves, but they sure gave our team a run for our money.

Because he was in such demand as a pilot, Dunigan finished his missions before the rest of us. While he was waiting to return home, he played on our squadron's baseball team as a catcher - he was great. It wasn't until then that we found out he had played baseball while he was in college at the University of Wyoming.

A skeet range had been set up for the gunners to practice. It actually turned out to be kind of a recreational activity. It was a fun time for a bunch of guys to get together and see who could outshoot the other. I got to be a pretty good shot, and for a while there I was the one to beat.

The Enlisted Men's Club was a place to hang out and drink. The problem was, there wasn't much of anything decent to drink. Mostly, all that was available was the local Italian stuff. There was Italian whisky that we called moonshine. The typical drink was about half a glass of that Italian whisky and the other half was Italian dark vermouth. There was no ice. Our flight surgeon, Doc Remley, advised us not to drink the stuff; he said it was poison. Nobody ever died from drinking it, but there were plenty of deadly hangovers. Sometimes we could get a real cheap grade of Italian gin. It was drinkable if we could get a hold of some grapefruit juice to mix with it. There was some awful tasting Italian wine that reminded me of drinking vinegar. Later in life, I never was able to cultivate much of a taste for wine. No matter how expensive the bottle, it always seemed to taste like that cheap Italian stuff.

Officers could buy American whisky; I think they were rationed a quart every month. None of our officers drank, so it was tempting to ask one of them to buy a bottle for us every now and then, but we knew better than to ask. They looked out for us; and besides, Dunigan would have been disappointed in us for asking.

We were rationed two beers and two cokes a week. I usually traded my coke tickets for beer. The beer came in crates packed in saw dust to keep the bottles from breaking. I remember that beer sure tasted good especially if the cold weather had cooled it down real good. For some reason, that beer would foam up every time one was opened. You had to learn to be quick or half of your beer foamed away. It only took one or two times to learn - I was a quick learner.

A pool table sure would have been nice, but there wouldn't have been room for one. Several of us did ask for a dart board, but nothing ever came of it. For lack of anything else to do, a lot of gambling went on in the bar. There seemed to always be a crap game going on, and a lot of the guys liked to play poker. All the gambling seemed to be pretty good natured; I don't remember anybody accusing anybody of cheating or anything like that. As far as I know, nobody lost their paychecks. I wasn't much into gambling, but I did enjoy a friendly game of gin rummy once in a while. Dunigan would sometimes come by our tent and play rummy with us.

Maybe there wasn't a pool table or dart board in the enlisted club, but we did have a piano. I was real excited the first time I saw it and inquired about when the music started. Sadly, I was informed that there wouldn't be any unless I could make it myself. I soon learned that the NCO in charge of our club was very possessive of that piano. I guess, in the past, somebody had come through who could play, and he was hoping that would happen again. Until another player showed up, he would let the officers borrow it and lug it over to their club in the evenings. A couple of the officers could play, but the loud and drunken singalongs drowned out the music. The officers had to have the piano back the next morning, or the NCO went looking for it; he wouldn't just let them keep it until he needed it back. Guess he figured he might not ever get it back. I don't recall how it happened that the piano ended up in the enlisted club and not the officers. The whole time I was there, we never did get anybody in who could play - that sure would have been nice.

Sunday morning was ration day; everybody reported to the supply room and lined up with their hat in hand. As we passed through the line we were able to pick up our supplies: soap, shaving cream, razor blades, candy bars, etc. At the end of the line you paid up and also received and paid for your beer and coke tickets. I didn't smoke, but I always got my ration because cigarettes were better than money for trading with the Italians. I remember one time a shipment of pocket knives came in. There weren't enough for everybody, so only every seventh man got one. Even if the seventh man didn't want the pocket knife he took it because it could quickly be sold or traded.

There were several church services for all the different denominations. I attended whenever I could, but a lot of Sundays I was flying. Sunday was just another day when you were in a combat zone. The Easter I was there, it was reported that every single man in the squadron went to church; the weather must have had everybody grounded. There was a chaplain available at all times if anyone felt the need to talk with him. I know, after rough and bloody missions, guys sometimes went to the chaplain to try to find some consolation. If a guy got a "Dear John" letter or was having family problems, the chaplain tried to give him some words of encouragement.

It wasn't long before we were using our heater to do a little cooking of our own. Mostly we heated up water in our canteen cup and mixed in beef bouillon cubes or hot chocolate mix from our K-Rations. I remember sitting around the heater sipping my hot drink, feeling right at home. We even boiled eggs; there were a few local farmers who would trade cigarettes for fresh eggs. Since all we ever got in the mess hall were powdered eggs, those fresh, hard-boiled eggs were a real treat.

Somehow, the guys in my tent all got to be friendly with one of the Italian workers on the base who we called "Old Mike." He kept us supplied with wine for our tent. What he got us was just slightly a step up from what they served at the club. It still tasted like vinegar to me; consequently, I only drank wine if there was absolutely nothing else available. In return, we gave him candy and other treats for his kids. Old Mike looked out for us.

At first I thought the local Italians must be smoking fanatics since they were so interested in our American cigarettes. Soon, I learned that they wanted them to trade on the black market. It seemed that cigarettes were much more valuable than money when trading for what few items were available to them. It was illegal for us to sell our cigarettes to the Italians, but everybody did it; we sold ours to Old Mike.

Two or three times a week a movie was shown in the Group Briefing Room. I attended a few, but usually I preferred to read. There was a pretty good selection of books and magazines in the day room. On occasion, there was a boxing match. Flight crew members weren't allowed to box, but it was fun to be a spectator. Some of those guys were pretty good. Once, a black service squadron came through and put on a floor show for us. It was silly with some terrible singing and pitiful dancing, but we all enjoyed it and had a few laughs. We were desper-

L to R: Jack Taylor, Michael Joyce (with broom), Tucker, and Clyde Dwight.

ate for any kind of entertainment, and the show proved to be a nice distraction.

We had to keep our tents clean and do our own laundry. Some of us would wash out a few things in a tub outside the tent and hang them to dry on a make-shift clothes line. That was not a pleasant task when the weather was freezing cold. When it was raining, we tried to hang up our clothes in the tent which was a real hassle. Sometimes, for a small fee, some rations, or cigarettes, we would hire one of the local farm families to do our laundry.

I had always grown up with a family dog, so I took notice of a couple of dogs that ran loose around the area and would often stop and pet them. One was a small, friendly, black and white mutt. I did notice that he was only friendly to guys in uniform; he would have nothing to do with the civilians. I soon learned that, while we were in crew training in Alexandria, the mutt befriended one of the crews and quickly became their mascot. They couldn't decide on a name, so they just went with "Alphabet." I guess they figured that would cover all names.

One of the guys on the crew, a fellow named Barwick

from Ft. Lauderdale, told me the dog traveled on the train with them to Lincoln, Nebraska, and that Alphabet actually flew over to Italy with them in a B-17. He told me they even rigged up an oxygen mask for the dog - now, that would have been a sight.

Unfortunately, Alphabet's crew went down in Russia where they were detained for quite awhile before being sent directly back to the states. Poor Alphabet; he waited at the runway for days for his crew to return. He never took up with another crew; he was kind of an orphan and just wandered from tent to tent.

It turned out that Barwick was able to get word to the Red Cross about Alphabet. Fortunately, someone in the Red Cross relayed a message to a friend of Barwick's who was still in Italy. When the friend went home, he took Alphabet back to the states with him and delivered the dog to Barwick's family in Ft. Lauderdale.

There was another little black and white dog whose story wasn't quite as glamorous as Alphabet's. The little dog was just a local mutt who wandered in and took up with a crew - they named him Flak. All was well for Flak until his adopted crew was hit by flak and went down with no survivors. Because he was such a cute and friendly dog, he was quickly adopted by another crew. A short time later, that crew went down as the result of flak; again, with no survivors. Well, poor old Flak couldn't find a new home after that; in fact, guys would shoo him away from their tents and even throw rocks at him. The poor dog just couldn't understand why the usually friendly crews suddenly wanted nothing to do with him. A couple of the cooks took pity on the shunned mutt and took him in.

The whole time I was there, I had gotten used to the Italians and had even learned to exchange a few words with them. One morning, shortly before I left to come home, I went to the mess hall and all the Italians were gone. There wasn't an Italian anywhere on the base; overnight, they had vanished. The explanation we got was that a couple of them were caught under the stage area of briefing operations, attempting to bug it.

The Italians had been replaced with Polish soldiers - now that was a sight. They were in full uniform and appeared to be part of an active Polish Army. They had escaped Poland before the German and Russian occupation. I was told that we even had Polish soldiers fighting with us on the front lines. They were good workers, but I never heard one of them say a word - we really missed Old Mike.

A Mission

Chapter 16

Making of a Mission

We soon learned that the 97th had the reputation of having the best ground crews in the 15th Air Force. It was a great relief to witness those men in action because the ground crew was our lifeline. I never saw anybody on the ground who wasn't as gung ho and dedicated as we were. They worked long hours, often late into the night, and took great pride in the success of their planes. It was a sad day for the ground crew if one of their planes had to turn back from a mission because of mechanical failure; it was an even sadder day if their plane didn't return at all.

There were probably about a dozen planes per squadron. Each B-17 had a crew chief and four mechanics. The aircraft mechanics kept the engines repaired and running smoothly. The ground crews worked tirelessly to make sure our Fortresses were ready for every mission. They checked and rechecked to see that every fuel tank was filled to the top, our tires were fully inflated, and our oxygen tanks were recharged. There were communications people who made sure our radios and intercom system were in good working order. A munitions crew handled all the bombs and ammunition. When a plane returned with battle damage, the sheet metal crew worked tirelessly to get her back in the sky. It took a lot of coordination by the ground crew chiefs and the flight line chiefs to get hundreds of planes ready for a mission.

I don't recall any jealousy or anything like that between

the flight crews and the ground crews. If anybody on the ground complained about us having a better deal all they had to do was go to operations and sign up to become a gunner. They would be taken out to the gunnery range and trained. All they had to do was learn to fire a .50 caliber machine gun. As far as I know, nobody decided to make the transition.

I always felt a little sorry for everybody on the ground. The flight crews were over there and out as soon as we flew our required combat missions. I was only in Italy for less than a year. Now, it was a rough year, but I was motivated to get in as many missions as possible and get out of there. Folks on the ground often stayed as long as three years.

The B-17 was an amazing airplane. Ask anybody who ever flew in one and they will you tell you it was the best aircraft ever built. Crews had the utmost respect and confidence in the Seventeens. If there ever was a plane built that would get you there and back, it was a B-17. The Fortresses were designed to fly up to an altitude of 30,000 feet with a maximum range of 1,800 miles and an air speed of up to 300 miles an hour. They could take off with three tons of bombs, almost 3,000 gallons of fuel, 13 guns, and 10 crew members. The four Wright Cyclone engines were very powerful and reliable. Many B-17s made it back on three engines and occasionally even on two.

The B-17 could take so much abuse from antiaircraft guns, better known as flak, and from enemy fighter jets. Many a B-17 was known to make it back even with holes big enough for a man to jump through. As long as the controls and engines were in working order, the Fortress would almost always get you home.

Personally, those big, heavy old birds probably gave me a false sense of security. I remember feeling like I really was inside a fortress which was being guarded by thirteen .50 caliber machine guns. Along with my very competent crew and outstanding pilot, I felt like we stood a good chance of making it back. Obviously, I saw some go down, but I always believed

the one I was in was going to keep flying. No matter how rough the flak got, I was usually pretty confident that big, old bird was going to hold together and get us back.

Generally, we stayed with one plane as long as it didn't get shot up too bad or had mechanical problems. Since both happened often, we would have to leave our plane behind for the ground crew to patch up and repair. It was best not to get too attached to any one plane because most of the time we just had to take off in whatever was available.

The Fortresses often had pretty memorable names that were displayed, along with some matching art work, on the nose. Without doing some research, I can only recall the names of two. The first was the *Kwitchubitchin* which was the first plane we all flew together in as a crew. She was good to us and brought us back safe and all in one piece. We immediately took a liking to her and claimed her as our own. How fitting that it was the *Kwitchubitchin* that Dunigan was able to make an emergency landing in Yugoslavia when we were shot down. How could I ever forget her?

One of the oldest planes in the squadron was *Magnetic Maggie*. She got her name because she seemed to attract flak like a magnet but never bad enough to put her out of commission. I remember flying with her a couple of times.

Not all planes had names. We were assigned to a plane by its serial number, never its nose name. Usually the flight crew named the planes, but sometimes it was the ground crew who came up with an appropriate name. Think about it, the ground crew had plenty of time to decorate the nose of any one of the planes they were assigned to. They spent hours maintaining the plane, so why not name it, too.

Of course, we liked the newer G models because they were roomier, especially for me back in the tail. I used to kid the guys about having enough room to dance around back in the tail of those G models. But we didn't mind flying the F models because they were warmer and faster. They didn't have a chin turret to add extra drag. Some crews liked having the two extra guns provided in the chin turret of the G model.

Planes needed to have some kind of markings so they could be identified by other groups. So began the practice of painting identification marks on planes to include the wing, group and squadron. In the 15th Air Force, all Fifth Wing aircraft carried a big Y on their vertical stabilizer. The tail insignia for the 97th bomb group was a black Y in a white triangle. Squadrons were identified by the last number following the serial number under the white triangle.

We arrived without a left-waist gunner because we had to leave Kenneth Snow behind as ordered. Whenever we flew a mission, we were assigned a substitute gunner just for that mission; one day Earl Whit flew as our substitute. When we came back, he asked all of us gunners if he could be our regular at left-waist. He said he had flown with a lot of other crews; he thought we were the best he had seen. We asked Dunigan, and he said if it was alright with us it was a go. Whit fit right in and happily became a permanent member of our crew.

Soon after we settled in our tent it became apparent that Vignes, our radio operator, was a slob. Also, he was always rubbing somebody the wrong way because he ran his mouth a lot. You know the type, finding fault with everything we did and constantly making sarcastic remarks. The rest of us agreed that he had to go; so we all got together and went over to Dunigan's tent. Dwight, being our spokesman, pleaded our case. As expected, Dunigan went right along with us. He promptly went to the Orderly Room and told the operations officer to take Vignes off our crew and out of our tent. It didn't seem to bother Vignes at all; I kinda suspected he was used to that kind of treatment. We never did get a permanent radio operator after

that; we just got whoever. That was kind of a shame because, in spite of all his faults, Vignes was a good radio operator.

The ten men who made up your crew were the most important people in your life. You lived with those guys, partied with them, worked with them, and faced death with them. As a crew, we pretty much stuck together. None of us got too friendly with any of the other crews. That seemed to be the way it was with everybody. I know, for me, when I heard that we lost a plane and some or all of the crew, I didn't want to know them personally. If I lost a buddy, I wanted to be with him.

On every mission, I was always so thankful for our crew. The teamwork and dedication displayed by each and every one of those guys was second to none. There was no doubt in my mind that they were each going to play a huge role in getting us all back alive. My biggest fear wasn't of dying - my biggest fear was letting my crew down. There may have been ten of us, but when we got in that plane and prepared for takeoff, we were one. Every time, as we approached enemy territory and I crawled back to my position in the tail, I would always be comforted by this thought: "If I die today, it will be with some of the bravest and finest young men I've ever known."

Chapter 17

The Weather

The weather played a huge role in the whole flying operation. Weather patterns over the Alps and the mountains surrounding the base were usually the culprit. Sometimes we would be grounded for days because of bad weather. Sitting around, doing nothing, and waiting for the weather to clear could be very frustrating. Remember, we wanted to get in the air so we could complete our 35 missions and get out of there ASAP.

Even more frustrating was getting all prepared, sitting in your plane waiting for takeoff clearance, and then a red flare would signal the mission had been scrubbed because of the weather. Even more stressful was actually getting in the air and forming up, then getting called back because of weather. Taking off with a full load of bombs was dangerous enough, but having to land with bombs on board was even more hazardous.

Talk about some disgruntled flyers. I don't think I can ever remember more fussing and cussing going on than when riding back to the base after a scrubbed mission; all that time and effort wasted. The ever important "completed missions count" would have to wait for another day.

The lead ship in a formation was usually fitted with radar which we referred to as "The Mickey Ship." The ball turret had to be removed and replaced with the radar dome which made some crews a little nervous because they lost two guns. The equipment wasn't very refined but could be very helpful when dropping bombs in fog or cloud cover. Radar was also helpful when dropping bombs on a target protected by smoke pots.

We never liked flying through fog. With the visibility cut down to a minimum, the pilots had to loosen up the formation to avoid mid-air collisions. As soon as we were out of the soup, it was always scary to see just how scattered the formation had gotten. As soon as the skies cleared, pilots hurried to get back in formation. It wasn't unusual for German fighters to be waiting on the other side of a fog bank hoping to get a shot at a lone Fortress that had gotten separated from the formation in the fog.

Of course, mud was a problem everywhere. It was a constant battle to keep it out of our tents because our boots would bog up to our ankles. Vehicles would slip and slide and get stuck. As far as flying, our landing field wasn't in the best of shape, so mud could accumulate on the tires during takeoff. When high altitude was reached, the mud would freeze and could hide any damage to the landing gear.

During one particular landing, our right tire had been hit with a piece of flak; the damage went undetected because of the frozen mud. When Dunigan touched down, the tire blew, causing the plane to veer to the right. Dunigan gunned the left engines to get us off the runway as fast as possible and out of the way of the plane landing behind us; we ended up mired in a field of mud. The ground crew had to come out with a six-by to pick up the crew and then had to lay cleat tracks to pull the plane out.

The winter of '43-44 was cold; we had some snow, but no blizzards or anything that shut us down. As far as I know, the snow didn't interfere with any of the missions. Building snowmen and having snowball fights seemed to top my memory of snow in a combat zone.

In front of our officer's tent. Top L to R: Dwight, Tucker, Nisula, Dunigan, McQuistion. Bottom L to R: Garrison, Taylor, Joyce, Whit.

Back: Dwight & Nisula; Front: Tucker & Taylor

Chapter 18

Briefing

You knew if you were going to be flying the next day because a roster was posted the evening before. Even so, you were never prepared when the CQ came around and knocked on, or just jerked open, your tent door and hollered out the names of everybody flying that day. Keep in mind, the time was anywhere from 02:30 to 04:30 hours. You'd jump up, pull on your coveralls, grab your mess kit and run to the mess hall to eat. After breakfast, you'd haul ass back to your tent, put up your mess kit, grab your Colt 45, and head to briefing.

Before every mission, all the crews assembled in the Group Briefing Room. In some outfits only the officers attended, but in the 97th we were all included. It made more sense to have us there and hear everything firsthand instead of the pilot having to brief the enlisted men later. Personally, I think it was good for the morale of the enlisted men. The crews all sat together which gave the groups the opportunity to hear their fate as one.

The first order of business was for a group briefing officer to pull down a map of central Europe. Black ribbon marked the course to the target. Often the reaction was neutral, but sometimes, if it was a known rough target, there would be groans from the audience. A group operations officer would then divert our attention to a screen where he went over an aerial photo of the target. He went on to inform us about what to expect as far as flak and enemy fighters. An intelligence officer would brief us on the best route of escape if we crash landed or bailed out. We were always briefed by a meteorologist about what weather conditions to expect on the way and over the target.

The last order of business in a briefing was a time hack. It was important for everybody to synchronize their watches because, on a mission, timing was of utmost importance. The briefing officer would start the countdown and, when the correct time was reached, he would call "Hack" and everybody would push their winding stems back in.

A sound I will never forget was the scraping of the metal stools against the concrete floor as all the men quickly rose at the end of briefing. Our seats were discarded 500-pound bomb tail-fin protectors. It seemed to be part of the ritual to see just how loud we could scrape those stools before departing for the mission.

As the gunners moved toward the waiting trucks, the pilots got together with the operations planner to work out their positions in the formation. The navigators, bombardiers and radio operators all got together with their lead person to discuss their issues for the mission.

We always carried our identification card with us on every mission.

I AM AN AMERICAN.
PLEASE TAKE ME TO THE NEAREST AMERICAN OR BRITISH MISSION,
OR TO THE NEAREST RUSSIAN MILITARY AUTHORITY.

THANK YOU.

JESTEM AMERYKANIN.
PROSZE ODPROWADZIĆ MNIE DO NAJBLISZEGO POSELSTWA
AMERYKAŃSKIEGO ALBO ANGIELSKIEGO, ALBO, DO NAJBLISZEGO
WLADZA ROSYJSKIEGO WOJSKA.

DZIĘKUJE SERDECZNIE.

POLAND

JÁ JSEM AMERIČAN!
PROSIM VÁS ZAVEĎTE MNE K NEJBLIŽŠÍ AMERICKÉ NEB BRITSKÉ
MISI, NEBO K NEJBLIŽŠÍMU RUSKÉMU VOJENSKEMU ÚŘADU.

DĚKUJI!

CZECHOSLOVAKIA

JA SAM AMERIKANAC.
MOLIM POVEDITE ME DO NAJBLIŽE AMERIKANSKI ILI ENGLESKE MISIJE,
ILI DO NAJBLIŽE RUSKE VOJNICKE VLASTI.

HVALA

YUGOSLAVIA

AMERIKAI VAGYOK
KÉREM KISÉRJEN EL A LEGKÖZELEBBI AMERIKAI VAGY ANGOL,
BIZOTTSÁGHOZ AVAGY A LEGKÖZELEBB LEVO OROSZ KATONAI
HATÓSAGHOZ.

KÖSZÖNÖM SZÉPEN

HUNGARY

ICH BIN AMERIKANER.
BITTE BRINGEN SIE MICH ZUR NÄCHSTEN AMERIKANISCHEN ODER
ENGLISCHEN MISSION ODER ZUR NÄCHSTEN RUSSISCHEN BEHÖRDE.

VIELEN DANK

AUSTRIA & GERMANY

These phrases were folded inside our identification cards.

After briefing, we'd load up in the back of a six-by for a quick ride out to the crew shack. There, we each had a storage bin where we kept a big canvas bag that held our flying clothes and electric suit, parachute harness and pack, "Mae West" life jacket, oxygen mask, and any other equipment. Our escape kit contained a compass, folding bayonet, maps, matches, and a few first aid supplies. I still have that compass today.

Before heading to the plane, each crew member checked out a sealed pouch with $50 American money which we stored in a zipper compartment in our pants leg. The money was to be used as bribe money if shot down. We were told that we could even write an IOU if we thought that would help save us. Having bribe money could be especially helpful in Yugoslavia because of the Partisan support. I actually heard about the American Government paying up on some IOUs after the war.

Then it was back in the truck for the ride out to the plane. As the driver approached a hardstand, he would shout out the last three numbers of the plane's serial number. If it was your assigned plane you would yell out for him to stop, jump out, and lug your awkward equipment bag to the waist door. You would find both pilots and the flight engineer walking around the plane making a pre-flight check. Shortly before takeoff, a jeep passed by, and the driver tossed out a box of K-rations. One last ritual before hopping aboard was to ease off to the side of the aircraft and take a final whiz.

Often the ground-crew chief would say something like, "Bring my plane back in one piece." Forget about us; he just wanted to

Drawing of Hitler found on the back of a Group Christmas Card

make sure we took care of his plane.

When we got the green light from the tower everybody hopped in and prepared for takeoff. Again, both pilots and flight engineer went through a cockpit check before starting the engines. I'll never forget the sound of those powerful Wright engines as we taxied out and got in line for takeoff.

Chapter 19

Dressing for Combat

You actually got dressed for the mission as the planes were forming up. The biggest concern was staying warm at high altitudes where the temperature could reach 50° below zero. Deaths from hypothermia and serious injuries from frostbite were a very real concern. As cumbersome as they were, our heated suits were a life saver. All the parts snapped together and plugged into one another so the current from the plane's 12-volt electrical system could move throughout the suit. Our brogans would not fit on over the electric booties, but we kept them nearby. If we went down, the plan was to snap our brogans to our parachute harness. Our feet would be in sad shape if we went down and only had our booties to trudge around the countryside in.

On our hands, we usually started with silk gloves, then the electric gloves, and finally fur-lined leather gloves. Our heads were covered with a leather helmet with built-in ear phones. Even our oxygen masks were plugged in to keep them from freezing up. Next, we strapped on our Colt 45 shoulder holster. On top of all that, we put on our flight jacket. If that wasn't enough, we wore a rubberized "Mae West" life vest that could be inflated if needed. Last, we strapped on our parachute harness. We didn't wear our parachute, but kept it nearby, so it could be clipped on quickly if we needed it. Our flak vest and helmet stayed in the plane near our combat station. We only put them on when we were in flak areas because the vest weighed 22 pounds. Even if they had weighed 100 pounds, everybody

would have worn them because they offered protection that could save lives. It wouldn't be long before I found out just what a lifesaver they were.

Chapter 20

Flying In Formation

Once the green flare was given, planes began to taxi out to the runway for takeoff. As soon as the first plane broke the ground, another immediately started its takeoff roll. The planes were lined up on the runway in order by the position they were to fly that mission. It took awhile to get everybody in the air. Once that was done, the next order of business was to get into formation.

Getting into formation could be particularly dangerous especially in bad weather. Large numbers of bombers would be circling, gaining altitude while waiting for all the planes to get airborne. The sky could get pretty crowded which was really dangerous in fog or low cloud cover. The goal was to be formed up by the time we crossed the Adriatic Sea.

Depending on the size of the mission, we would form up into squadrons, groups, and wings. The 97th Bomb Group would usually fly four squadrons of seven planes each. The seven planes in a squadron would form up into a box or diamond shape. Each position in the formation had a name. Obviously, the plane at the top of the diamond was "lead" and the one at the bottom was the "tail." The lead plane always carried the highest ranking pilot. The tail was the least desirable position because that plane was most vulnerable to an attack by German fighters.

Taking off could be a very dangerous part of the mission, especially in bad weather. Remember, we were fully loaded with fuel and usually ten 500-pound bombs, hundreds of pounds of .50-caliber ammunition and ten men. Because we had to take off at such a rapid pace, there was always the danger of planes colliding. Getting into and staying in formation was also dangerous business. Occasionally, planes collided in mid air which resulted in catastrophic loss of lives. Many of the rookie pilots just didn't have the experience needed to hold those huge, heavy B-17s steady while flying in such close proximity.

I had a personal experience with one of those inexperienced pilots. On that particular mission, there was a rookie pilot flying in a lower position behind us. When the flak got heavy or if enemy fighters were spotted, he would come up way too close; I could look him and the co-pilot in the eye. I called Dunigan and asked him to call the pilot and tell him to back off. Well, he did drop back; but just as soon as conditions started getting rough again, he was right back on our butt. I called Dunigan again and reported the situation. He suggested, "Wobble your guns at him, Tuck; show him you mean business." Well, that's exactly what I did, and he backed off alright; and he stayed back...way back. Guess it took looking down the barrels of two .50-caliber machine guns for that guy to realize that he better stay off our butt.

I never witnessed it, but I heard horror stories of planes veering out of formation on a bomb run. After "bombs away," the bombs from a higher plane would hit a lower plane with disastrous results. Either plane could have been out of formation, but it was the lower plane that took the hit. What a tragic way for ten men to lose their lives to "friendly fire."

The main reason for flying in formation was for protection against enemy fighters. As we would get closer to the target and into unfriendly skies, the pilots would tighten up the formation to leave as little space between the planes as possible. That maneuver made it more difficult for the German fighters to single out a plane to attack. The tight formation also concentrated the firing power of the gunners; likewise, if the planes were in a tight formation as they passed over the target, the bombs would concentrate in on the target.

On the way up to our targets in northern Italy was the

city of Udine. Located there was a German fighter base with Italian pilots. As many times as we passed Udine going back and forth, those fighters never challenged us because we were always in tight formation. The one time they did take off, we had a straggler. Several of the German ME-109s took off and headed for the lone straggler. When our group-lead pilot saw what was happening, he told us to do a three-sixty to go back and pick up our straggler. As soon as the Italian fighter pilots saw us coming, they headed straight back to their base; they knew not to mess with us.

Chapter 21

Fighter Escorts

We were fortunate beyond belief to have fighter escorts to and from our targets. Early on in the war, unprotected bomber groups were slaughtered by the German fighters. At that time, some of the bull-headed brass thought B-17s had enough fire power to defend themselves against the enemy fighters.

Just one example of the slaughter was the Eighth Air Force raid on the Schweinfurt ball-bearing plants. Sixty B-17s were lost in that one raid - that's 600 men. You have to also take into consideration that some of the planes made it back with dead men and the seriously wounded on board. The untold losses of that mission may have played a part in making some of the top brass rethink the need for fighter escorts on bombing missions.

Dunigan knew what time to expect the escorts, so he would radio the crew, "Start looking for our fighter escort. They're in the area." By golly, in no time at all you could look around and see our "little friends" zooming into sight.

Even though we knew to expect them, the fighter pilots didn't want to take any chances of being mistaken for an enemy. The P-38 Lightening was the easiest to distinguish because of its boom; but just to be safe, the pilots would approach with their bellies turned toward us.

The P-51 Mustang looked more like the German ME-109. The pilots never came in pointing their noses at us; instead, they would make sure we got a good silhouette view of them before they got into firing range. We liked seeing the P-51s because they were faster and had a longer range. They were equipped with 75-gallon drop tanks under each wing.

Our favorite escorts were the P-51s from the all black Tuskegee Fighter Group. During briefings, when it was announced that our escort was to be the 332nd, we all cheered. They had something to prove, and we were delighted to be on the receiving end.

Eagle eye Garrison, our co-pilot, always scrutinized the fighter escorts real close. On one mission, we hadn't approached the target yet when Garrison reported, "That P-38 doesn't look right; keep an eye on him. I'm going to see what I can find out." In a minute he came back on, "All our P-38s are accounted for; he's not supposed to be here." Dunigan contacted the commander of the fighter escorts and reported the strange P-38 flying opposite our group. Instantly, the rogue fighter peeled off out of sight.

That practice was a slick way for the Germans to report our air speed and altitude to their flak gunners as we approached the target. The Germans were known to repair our downed planes to be used to infiltrate our missions. It was even suspected that one of our missions was penetrated by a rogue B-17.

By the time I got into the war, fighter escorts were the rule; I don't remember going on a single mission without them. Our fighter pilots kept the German fighters occupied and engaged, which kept them off our butts. What a welcomed sight it was to see our "little friends" glide in beside us on our way to the target; likewise, it was a big let down to see them ease off and out of sight when we got closer to home.

Chapter 22

I P- Initiation Point

During a bomb run, we never flew directly to the Initiation Point; instead, we made a wide turn to approach the target. The bomb run started when we turned on the IP - it usually lasted about three to five minutes. When the bombardier turned his bomb sight on, that action automatically took over control of the aircraft. That's when the bombardier would announce, "Bomb-bay doors opening."

The radio operator physically looked to make sure the doors were open. After he acknowledged the bomb-bay doors were open, there was nothing to do then but fly straight and level. The pilot couldn't vary altitude, direction or airspeed. We were a sitting duck until the bombs were dropped because the pilot couldn't take any evasive actions. Of course, the Germans knew that, so that was when the flak was the heaviest.

As soon as the bombardier saw that the cross hairs on the bomb sight were lined up, he released the bombs and hollered, "Bombs away!"

Immediately after that, the radio operator would look to make sure all bombs had cleared; then he would yell, "All bombs away!"

The bombardier then informed us, "Bomb-bay doors closing."

The radio operator would then verify and conclude with, "Bomb-bay doors closed. Let's get the hell out of here!"

As soon as the bombs dropped, the plane lurched upwards. That lurch was a sure sign that we were no longer

carrying a bomb load. That was always a welcomed relief because now the pilot could once again begin taking evasive action against the flak. Unfortunately, the German fighters were usually circling, waiting for us to get out of the heaviest flak over the target.

Sometimes, depending on the target, we would drop a leaflet bomb in addition to our regular bombs. The leaflets were to warn the German civilians that delayed-action bombs had been dropped. The strategy was to keep the German people away from the bombed sight as long as possible. If they couldn't return to their jobs, production would be slowed down.

Chapter 23

Enemy Fighters and Flak

On a mission, one of our two worst enemies was the German fighters. The machine-gun fire from enemy fighters could take down a Fortress and all ten men aboard. The German fighter pilots were often quite skilled and were willing to take great risks to take down the heavily armed Fortresses. The enemy fighter pilots aimed for our engines, but machine-gun bullets ripping through an aircraft could do massive damage and devastating personal injury or death.

If German fighter pilots happened upon a group that wasn't flying in tight formation, they were known to pick a weak spot and fly through it. Their strategy was to get the bombers to spread out and possibly separate one from the group; a lone bomber was easy prey. Part of that tactic was also to tempt the gunners to fire at the passing German fighter; in doing so, there was a possibility that fire from one B-17 could hit another.

The Messerschmitts, or ME-109s, were a constant threat. The Focke-Wolf, or FW-190, usually approached from straight ahead and above. The Fortresses had a weak spot in the nose section, and the Germans knew it. The FW-190 pilots would slowly roll and come up under us so their armor-plated bellies would protect them from our fire.

The crews who flew later in the war were very fortunate to have fighter escorts to help keep the enemy fighters at bay. Our fighter escorts made sure the enemy fighters couldn't get to us without a dog fight first. The German fighters were always a concern, especially if your plane was lagging behind the formation. A lone bomber, with no protection in sight, was an easy target for the enemy.

Once, we were left lagging behind. On our way home, we began to lose airspeed and altitude - not sure why. I just know that Dunigan was not about to let us lag behind and be a sitting duck for German fighters. The engines were designed to pull so many RPMs and just so much manifold pressure. If you exceeded the limits on either, you would burn up your engines. In order to keep up with the formation, he pulled 2500 RPMs and 45 inches of manifold pressure which, no doubt, exceeded the limits. When he landed and shut the engines down, that was it; those engines would never restart. That was a huge setback for the ground crew, but nobody said a word. Burning up those four engines could very well have saved our lives.

Late in the war the Germans developed a jet fighter. We had been briefed on the possibility of those jets showing up. Intelligence knew all about them and even had a very accurate artist rendition of the German Messerschmitt, or ME262. I was probably one of the first gunners in the 15th Air Force to get a shot at one.

The mission was to the Ruhlin oil refinery about 75 miles south of Berlin. We had just dropped our bombs and were coming off the target when I spotted one. It was way out of range when I called its position, "Seven o'clock level, going around toward nine!" Suddenly, I saw two more zooming straight in behind us. "Six o'clock level!" I shouted and started firing. About the same time the tail gunner in the plane next to us did the same.

There were four 30mm cannons in the nose of those jets. One burst hit the plane next to us and knocked the whole wing off. The mighty Fortress turned on its side and plunged toward Earth. It was later reported that seven chutes were seen. I was too busy firing to see if the tail gunner made it out.

Those three German fighter jets buzzed right on through our squadron. What threw us off was the way they flew right through their own flak smoke as we were coming off the target. No doubt, they were in touch with their ground gunners who

held their fire as their fighters passed.

I never saw any more of the German jet fighters, but some sightings were reported by the 8th out of England, and a few more were spotted by the 15th. The Germans were too late with their fighter jets; by the later stages of the war, we had pretty much dried up their fuel supply.

The Americans had also developed a jet fighter, the P-80. I never got to see one in action, but it was rumored to be much more maneuverable than its German counterpart. I talked to some guys who knew about a P-80 that had been brought to Italy for testing. They didn't actually get to see the plane because of tight security. They said you couldn't get within two miles of it.

I never did see any myself, but late in the war there were reports by fighter pilots of sighting what became known as foo fighters. They were reported to be silver-like objects that would follow an aircraft at a distance then dart out of sight at a high rate of speed. Some of the pilots reported that the objects appeared to be antimagnetic because when approached, they would instantly dart out of sight. Nobody ever had an explanation for them. After the war, the Germans and Japanese denied any knowledge of them, and the Americans denied any involvement. Personally, I don't have a clue, but it sure makes you wonder.

Every bomber crew's worst nightmare was flak. Flak was shot from cannons on the ground, and its intensity depended on how important the target was. When the flak started, we knew what size the shells were by the color of the smoke. If the smoke was black, it came from 88mm shells. We feared the 88s the most because they were known to be the most accurate. White smoke was from 105mm shells. Toward the end of the war, we started seeing 128mm blasts which also produced white smoke.

I only saw the brown smoke from 40mm shells once, and it came from American guns. Our mission was to fly over and bomb troop concentrations in northern Italy. The Americans

sent up a flak fence at 16,000 feet to let us know that we needed to bomb north of that fence.

As the Allied forces advanced toward Germany, the Nazis drew their resources closer in; so the longer the war went on, the heavier the concentration of flak. The Germans even had flak guns assembled on railroad cars which they moved closer to suspected targets. The higher we flew, the less accurate the flak was, but in turn, our bombing was less accurate. We did try to fly around the heaviest concentration, but once over the IP we couldn't do anything. The scariest thing about flak was you had no way of knowing where the next one was going to hit. There was nothing you could do but sit there and take it. With fighters, you could see them coming and at least return fire, but not with flak - you were a sitting duck.

Flak often did unbelievable damage to the bombers. The concussion from the blast would cause the plane to bounce around violently which could send the crew sprawling. If the blast was real close, the crew members could suffer concussions. Those big old birds could take unbelievable abuse and still get their crew back to safety. The problem was, often the Fortress brought back dead or seriously injured crew members. The B-17 might have survived the flak bursts; but often, some of the crew did not.

No one on board was trained to care for the wounded. We had a first-aid kit with morphine, and we all knew the importance of trying to stop the bleeding. My crew was very fortunate to have never had to deal with serious injuries on board. We were spared the gruesome sights and sounds of men laying in agony for untold hours until their plane returned to base. We never had to witness men injured so severely that they had no chance of surviving the trip home; so their crew members strapped them into a parachute, pulled the rip cord, and dumped them out, hoping the freezing temperatures on the way down would stop the bleeding, and maybe - just maybe - the injured flyer would be rescued.

On one rough mission, before reaching the target, we experienced some flak bursts in front of us, directly in our path. The next volley skipped us and burst directly behind our plane.

Immediately, another round burst, real close, out in front of us. Evidently, that was just too much for McQuistion, the bombardier, whose position was in the nose of the plane. He blurted out, "You SOBs! You haven't made one with my name on it!"

To which I immediately replied, "But Mac, what about the ones marked, 'To Whom It May Concern'?"

One attempt to cut down on the flak concentration was to dispense chaff into the air space. Chaff looked like little, foil strips just like icicles on a Christmas tree. The strips were loosely done up in little packages that would come apart when they were thrown out of the plane. There was a small well right behind the ball-turret gun with a hatch. One of the waist gunners would open the hatch and throw out one bundle every twenty seconds or so as we were approaching the target. The chaff was supposed to help foil the German radar. If anything, it caused the Germans to waste a lot of ammunition. Unfortunately, it didn't take them long to distinguish the chaff from our planes.

Once, toward the end of the war, near Munich, we witnessed three strange looking white smoke trails. From a distance, it looked like they were zigzagging but actually they were spiraling. From our intelligence report and an article in the *Stars and Stripes*, we later learned they were rockets fired from the ground. The rockets were estimated to be 12 feet long and would explode with a white phosphorous smoke. They produced flak that was much more lethal than the bursts from the cannons. Fortunately, that was the one and only time we ever saw the rocket-propelled flak.

Chapter 24

In Flight

Of course, our main objective on a mission was manning our duty stations and doing everything in our power to stay alive and ensure the safety of our crew members. However, there were other responsibilities that had to be taken care of and other activities that went on when we were in enemy skies.

In addition to dispensing chaff, one of the waist gunners was responsible for throwing out information leaflets. The handouts were filled with accurate information about the war. The goal was to let the German people know that the Germans were not winning the war. We used to joke about having the biggest paper route in the world because we dropped thousands of those booklets at a time.

Our navigator was responsible for doing oxygen checks every ten minutes when we were at altitudes above 10,000 feet. He would start with the tail. I would report, "Roger tail," then he would work his way up through the plane. Ours was a demand-type oxygen system which meant you had to breathe to get oxygen. A surprising number of lives were lost when guys fell asleep, causing their breathing to slow down; consequently, they died from lack of oxygen. We kept a real close check on each other when we were on oxygen.

Intelligence encouraged us to check out a K-20 camera to take along on missions and get shots of action or targets. If you were a taker, before a mission, a guy would deliver the camera to you at the plane. Just as soon as you landed, he was there to pick up the camera and rush it to the photo lab to get the pictures developed in time for interrogation. Occasionally, one of our crew would check out a camera and pass it around. I remember taking one or two pictures, but to tell you the truth, I was always too busy to fool with trying to take pictures. Besides, Intelligence had a photo reconnaissance P-38 that zoomed in after missions and took pictures.

All of our missions were long, but some could be as long as ten hours. Well, you gotta relieve yourself at some point during a mission. For that purpose, there were relief tubes installed in the plane; I even had one of my very own back in the tail. The tubes worked just fine until we got up in high altitude; then your pee froze as soon as it hit the tube. After that, the tube was useless and couldn't be used again until we got back down to low enough altitude for the pee to thaw out.

You were in real trouble if you had to poop because there weren't any facilities on board. Most flyers quickly got into a routine of doing their "morning constitution" in the afternoon because there just wasn't time in the morning before a mission.

On one mission, Halsey, our navigator, got the GIs. To avoid a real disaster, he did his business in a map box he had emptied. He quickly sealed the box up, cracked open the nose-access door, threw the box out, and commented with a grin, "I'd sure like to see the face of the Kraut who opens that box."

What a relief it was when we had dropped our bombs, made it out of enemy territory, and had come down from oxygen altitudes. All the gunners would gather and sit around on the radio room floor because it was a little warmer there. Finally, we could relax. Usually, we just shot the bull, but often the radio operator would tune in *Armed Forces Radio* for us. We could keep our headsets on and listen to the special broadcast that was on every afternoon which was dedicated to returning air crews. They played songs from *The Mediterranean Hit Parade* and even took requests. I remember the sheer delight of putting those headsets on and listening to some of the latest

THERE WAS ONLY a slight reshuffling in positions on the Mediterranean Hit Parade this week, and just one addition. *Rum And Coca Cola* and *Don't Fence Me In* continued to hold down the number one and two spots respectively, while *The Great Speckled Bird* moved up one notch from fourth place. This week's newcomer, in the number nine slot, is *One Meat Ball.* The line-up this week: THE LATEST

(1) Rum And Coca Cola, (2) Don't Fence Me In, (3) The Great Speckled Bird, (4) Somewhere On Via Roma, (5) I'll Walk Alone, (6) Don't Cry Baby, (7) You Can't Get That No More, (8) I'm Making Believe. (9) One Meat Ball, (10) You Always Hurt The One You Love.

ITALY - 1944

Newspaper article about Mediterranean Hit Parade. It was published weekly in the *Stars and Stripes.*

hits: *Lilly Marlene, Don't Fence Me In,* and *I'm Making Believe.*

That was also the time to dig out the K-rations if your stomach had settled down enough from the mission and you were hungry. Some items could be put up over the heater duct and defrosted enough to have yourself a pretty good snack. You either got a breakfast or lunch box which contained standard items: cans of cheese, potted meat, crackers, and concentrated fruit bars.

Landings were not nearly as stressful as takeoffs. The biggest concern was that everybody was in a hurry to get on the ground and out of the planes. We never had any incidents, but sometimes planes landed a little too close for comfort. When landing, first priority was given to any plane with injured on board or if a plane was crippled. Ambulances were standing by to transport the injured to the dispensary where minor injuries were treated by Doc Remley or a medic. If a pilot had injured crew on board, he had to determine the seriousness of the inju-

ries and decide if he should fly directly to Foggia where there was a hospital. If there were any dead on board, the pilot always took the bodies directly to Foggia.

I didn't even think about it at the time, but we never had to actually witness death or serious injuries up close and personal. Oh, we knew about death alright whenever we witnessed mid-air explosions and knew there were no survivors. We watched as planes were hit and fell apart, sometimes releasing jumpers - sometimes not. How fortunate we were to have been spared the anguish of witnessing dead and seriously injured flyers being removed from their planes.

Chapter 25

Interrogation

After a combat mission, we were picked up by a six-by and taken back to the equipment room to put up all our gear. On our way out, there was a medic sitting behind a little stand. Beside him lay a big ledger, a bottle of American whisky, and a shot glass. As we headed out the door, those interested stopped, signed their name in the ledger, and waited as the medic poured a shot. At first, I thought the shots were offered to help settle frazzled nerves; I soon learned that the intent was really to help loosen our tongues for interrogation.

After one particularly rough mission, I got a little carried away with the shots. I always took mine and Jack's because he didn't drink. Michael wasn't feeling too well that day so he let me have his. Somebody else offered me another, and I happily threw that one down too. Before I had time to take anybody up on another offer, Dwight took me by the arm and told me I had had enough. He led me out to the truck waiting to take us to interrogation. When we arrived and started climbing out, he pointed his finger at me and said, "Don't you say a damn word."

I was surprised that so many of the guys didn't want their shots after a combat mission. That was the only time enlisted men ever got American whisky. I thought it helped to relieve some of the tension; you had a lot of unwinding to do once you got on the ground. Through the years, I have continued to drink Scotch to help calm my nerves though I do add a few ice cubes and a splash or two of water.

Interrogation took place at Group Headquarters where

each crew met with an intelligence officer. If the weather was nice, we sometimes sat outside on picnic tables. Mostly, his questions were for the pilot about what position we flew, how the engine performed, etc. From all of us, he wanted to know about the intensity of enemy fighters and flak. From the bombardier, he inquired about the accuracy of the bomb run. Usually, the navigator stayed longer and went over his mission log with the intelligence officer.

Dedicated to one

who has served us faithfully for three hundred and twenty-three combat missions. Greeting us after each attack against the enemy with a warm and cheery smile. Sharing our hardships as well as our joys. Standing by us through Algerian heat, Tunisian dust and the sun and rain of Italy.

To

MISS ELZA « FLIP » FRAME, ARC

we

respectfully dedicate this volume

The Red Cross was set up just outside the interrogation area with coffee, donuts, and a roaring fire. Flip Frame was the name of the lady in charge. She had a warm and friendly personality and was always a welcomed sight after a mission. Naturally, I enjoyed the coffee and donuts, but mostly I enjoyed the friendly greetings from all the Red Cross ladies. Often, if we weren't just beat, some of us would linger awhile and stand around the fire where we enjoyed our refreshments and discussed the mission or just shot the bull.

FLIP'S FRYING FORTRESS

The bearer of this coveted document: S/Sgt. Kenneth S. Tucker

having completed 35 dangerous sorties to FLIP'S Italian-based do-nut stand (formerly of Africa) and 35 sorties over Schickelgruber territory, is hereby knighted an honorable member of FLIP'S FRYING FORTRESS!

Signed: Flip Frame
(Frying Fortress Pilotess)
AMERICAN RED CROSS

If a mission had been really tough, the only place I wanted to be was back in my tent. The stress of combat could completely zap me of energy and all I wanted to do was lay down and try to sleep; quite a few times I slept right through chow. If the mission wasn't too bad, I'd spruce up a little bit, go to chow, and then over to the club.

After one particularly long and tough mission, it was almost dark before interrogation was over. I was so weary I could hardly hold my head up. As I trudged back to the tent with my head down and my thumbs resting in the strap of my shoulder holster, I sensed two people approaching on the path. I didn't look up, but as I approached, they separated, stepped aside, and let me pass. I glanced up and realized that one was the group commander, a bird colonel, and the other was a visiting general. Neither of them said a word - they knew where I had been.

Welcomed Changes Off Base

Chapter 26

Foggia

It was pretty easy to get into Foggia. Guys could always catch a ride for the ten mile trip; it was pretty much standard procedure that a service truck never passed up a GI on the side of the road. If you weren't flying the next day, it was a good night to go into Foggia. I managed to make the trip at least once every week or two. One thing though - you never went alone.

Foggia had been hit pretty hard by bombs and had suffered some extensive damage, so there was very little to do. There were a few Italian bars that catered to the servicemen; but mostly, I remember hanging out at the USO Club. Somehow, we befriended a group of Australian gunners. I got a big kick out of their accents, and there was something about their free-spirited attitude that I liked. I was telling one of my Australian buddies how much we all enjoyed their company but didn't particularly care for the Royal Air Force (RAF) fellows. His response was, "Frankly old boy, we don't either."

Occasionally, our Australian friends visited our club, but mostly, we hung out at the Aussie Club. They had a sergeant who played the piano and sang; nothing professional, but it was entertainment.

A nice theater survived the bombings and had been leased by the American government. I can remember attending boxing matches, movies, and a few stage shows. One show I distinctly remember was the Broadway production of *Art Thou Cooking*, which was billed as having run on Broadway for two years. The productions were a nice distraction and well attended.

Foggia was the place to go to have your picture made to send home to the family. There were several photography shops, and all were known to do good work. For Christmas, my brother, Arthur, sent me an olive-drab vest so I could wear it over my uniform. To show him that I appreciated the gift, I had my picture made with the vest on over my Class Bs. The picture turned out right nice. I wore that vest for years after the war.

Photograph made in Foggia in vest my brother sent me for Christmas.

Chapter 27

Bari

Most everyone on my crew was motivated to fly as much as possible and get their missions completed; consequently, most of us stayed on the base and made ourselves available. However, after our tenth mission, when we were shot down, Jack, Mike and me decided maybe we should take a little break. The day we were shot down, we had a substitute togglier, Arthur Goodrich, who wanted to go with us; so the four of us requested a three-day pass to Bari.

Hitching a ride on a supply truck was never a problem, and we managed to make it as far as Cerignola. By the time we arrived, it was getting dark, and we knew we had better find a place to spend the night. Using hand gestures, we communicated to one of the locals that we needed a place to stay. He indicated that we should follow him. All was well, as we followed him down one street, turned up another, and finally ventured down an alley. The trip continued through a door that opened right off the alley, then up some stairs to another door. The local knocked on the door and went inside, leaving us standing in the hall.

You can imagine our shock when the door opened again, and there stood two American MPs holding Thompson submachine guns. Near them stood a local policeman and another guy who turned out to be an Italian undercover investigator. One of the MPs motioned for us to get against the wall and join the line up where he had already corralled our friendly local, a couple of older Italian women, and an older man.

The MP signaled for us to be quiet, and in a whispered voice, asked what we were doing there. I don't remember who did the talking for us, but it wasn't me. We all got out our ID cards and passes and explained that we were just looking for a place to spend the night. "You guys just stumbled in on one of the biggest black market operations in this part of the country. We're expecting the 'head man' any minute. You guys stay quiet," he whispered.

As I was leaning against the wall, I remember thinking that I was about to be gunned down by members of the Italian underworld. We had all heard stories about how ruthless and desperate those people were. Any minute now an unknown number of the Italian mafia was about to walk through that door. It was like something right out of a movie, and I was expecting some real action.

Sure enough, there was a knock at the door. I fully expected the door to open with the "head man" and his body guards swooping in. The door opened and the MPs grabbed this pitiful looking older Italian man and flung him against the wall with the rest of us - that was it.

One of the MPs told us not to spend the night in Cerignola but to hitch a ride about ten miles down the road where there was an American service unit. We wasted no time getting out of there and were soon picked up by a couple of Polish soldiers in a weapons carrier. Upon arrival at the unit, we were issued cots and told to report to the supply room and find a spot. Needless to say, we had had a pretty trying day and were ready to get some rest.

I set my cot up under a stairway. As we settled in and things began to quiet down, I began to hear some of the most beautiful music you could ever imagine. Someone appreciated classical music and had a shortwave radio playing real low. As I lay there listening to that beautiful music, I was suddenly overcome with loneliness. That music seemed to creep into my soul and find the place where my loneliness hid. I laid there for the longest time, listening to that music, feeling a million miles from home and all alone in the world.

The next morning, we arrived in Bari; and to my surprise, the city was in pretty good shape. It hadn't been torn up like so many other cities in Italy. We did some of the usual tourist stuff; we looked around in some of the shops and checked out some sidewalk cafes and bars.

Having learned from our previous mistake, we asked a GI about places to stay. He informed us that there were several nice Italian families in the area who would take in short-time boarders. He even knew of a real nice family who needed the rent money and assured us they were not involved in the black market.

The family turned out to be two older women and a little girl about six or seven years old. They seemed delighted to have us and went out of their way to make us feel welcomed. When we came in from a day of sightseeing, the women had wine, bread and cheese waiting for us. They tried their best to communicate with us, but mostly, we did a lot of smiling and nodding.

Postcard of Bari: Written on the back, "We walked down this street, not bad at all, in fact better than the picture shows."

We managed to communicate to the family that we wanted to get up at seven o'clock the next morning. I was pleasantly surprised when I was awakened by the giggling little girl tapping me on the shoulder and holding up seven fingers. She got a big kick out of us and thought everything we did was funny. Hearing a little girl's laughter was a welcomed change, even though it made me miss my sisters.

Chapter 28

Isle of Capri - Rest Camp

Usually, every crew was sent on R & R twice during their tour of duty. Back then it was called Rest Camp. Our crew just kind of laid low and didn't say anything because it was pretty much decided that we wanted to fly as much as possible, get our required missions done, and go home.

Doc Remley, our Flight Surgeon, supervised and scheduled the rest camp visits. Doc made it a point to check in with all the pilots to see if anybody on their crew was having any problems or had any signs of combat fatigue. If a concerned pilot reported that a particular crew member was having a rough go of it, Doc would schedule a rest camp visit for that individual. He was a real nice guy, and everybody thought the world of him. We all knew Doc Remley kept a real close check on us; he looked out for us. He took real good care of us, and we appreciated him for that.

I had flown 22 missions before there was a posting on the board that our crew would be going to The Isle of Capri for a week's rest. Usually several crews went at once, but for some reason, we were the only crew from our squadron on that particular trip.

The flight to Naples was aboard a B-17. Being passengers, rather than crew members, made for an interesting flight for all of us. Folks from Special Services were waiting to take us over to the harbor where we caught a ferry over to the Isle. Once on the Isle, we were greeted by a group of local men who all wanted to be our private tour guide.

Our first adventure was to board a cable car for the trip up a steep mountain to the main part of the village. Our tour guide spoke pretty good English and did his best to point out some of the high points of the Isle as we traveled up. About halfway up, he hesitated for a moment and changed his delivery to a very serious tone, "We've had pretty good luck with the safety of our cable car. The cable only breaks about every five years."

Cover of the tour guide pamphlet that I have saved all these years.

As expected, Michael asked, "When was the last time it broke?"

With a grin, the tour guide answered, "Exactly five years ago today."

The season was early spring so the weather was pleasant though still a little cool for swimming. The foliage was lush and green. What a pleasant change from the muddy, drab olive grove we had called home for the past several months. The fragrance from the flowers reminded me of the smells of the many gardenias and jasmine that grew in my mother's and grandmother's yards.

I was amazed by the topography of the place; just the way the residents had adapted to living on the sides of mountains was impressive. I was fascinated by the steep, winding mountain paths and terraced courtyards. The views, looking down on the harbor from high up on the side of mountains, were incredible. What a contrast to the ever flat terrain of northwest Florida where I grew up. At home, if I wanted to enjoy the view looking down on thc bay, my best vantage point would have been to climb to the top of the highest pile of oyster shells.

It appeared that all the hotels on the island had been taken over by the American Government. I was in for a shock when the enlisted men's accommodations turned out to be the beautiful Hotel PigannoVittoria. The views from every window were just beautiful. The rooms were spacious and so nice and clean; maids came in everyday to straighten up the room and make our beds. What a treat it was to have a bathroom with real plumbing.

Food choices were pretty limited because of the war, but I definitely remember the food being much better than our standard mess-hall rations. I remember a few fresh fruits and vegetables; best of all, there were fresh eggs and milk. It was such a pleasure to sit at individual tables and eat off of real plates while the waiters attended to our every need.

The hotel staff was friendly and went out of their way to make us feel welcomed. The hotel owner had a daughter who was probably about 12. We never saw her without her big German shepherd who never left her side; maybe that's why her father allowed her to walk freely around the hotel grounds. She spoke a few words of English and enjoyed trying to communicate with us. On occasion, she even accompanied us into town. I immediately took a liking to her because she reminded me of my sisters.

One morning, I met a guy who was staying at a hotel that had tennis courts. To my delight, he invited me over to play. What a treat, considering the only court I had ever played on was at the Browns back home in East Point. For the first time, I witnessed players who had form and style and looked so graceful. I was a pretty good tennis player and could hold my own, but style was something I did not possess. After watching some of those players, I promised myself that someday I would take lessons and improve my style. I never did, but I continued to enjoy playing tennis for many years.

I was thrilled to find a string ensemble, made up of three or four older Italian men, playing in the dining room every evening. They were accomplished musicians and played all the popular hits like *Lili Marleene* as well as their signature tune, *Isle of Capri.* Quite often, as I sat listening to their music, I couldn't help think of Lucille and wonder where she was and what songs she might be playing - sure made me wish I was sitting at a front row table in her audience.

Many young soldiers searched the streets of Capri hoping to find a beautiful young lady, as the story was told in the lyrics of the song. I remember hearing the song as a kid, but I certainly never thought I would visit the Isle of Capri.

Our tour guide set us straight about the lyrics, "Whoever wrote that song never set foot on Capri. There is no way a lady could be found beneath the shade of an old walnut tree like it says in the song. There have never been walnut trees anywhere on this island; and I'll tell you something else, nobody ever sailed with the tide in the morning like the song says. There are no tides on the Mediterranean." After that rendition, the song just didn't have the same appeal.

Regardless, there were no young girls to be found anywhere on the island; no doubt, parents kept their daughters behind closed doors - can't say I blamed them. The only young women I saw were prostitutes; and from the activities I witnessed, business was good.

Get two GIs together and they are going to find something to drink. Luigi's Bar, right off the village square, was a popular hangout for the enlisted men. As usual, we were served real cheap gin, whisky, and vermouth. Some good times were definitely had by all in Luigi's. Sure, the alcohol consumption fueled the fire, but the real energy came because young men were allowed to be just that - young and carefree. I don't remember any drunken brawls or fights, just a bunch of weary fighters escaping the stress of flying combat, if only for a few days.

One of our first excursions was a visit to the castle ruins of the Roman Emperor, Tiberius Caesar. The ruins sat on an overlook, high up on a mountain. Before starting to the top, we all bought cheap, tourist hats. Everybody turned up the brim in the front which made them look even more ridiculous. Those tacky hats provided a nice distraction from our uniforms and

Our donkey ride up to the Castle Ruins of Tiberius Caesar: Garrison and Tucker on the donkeys and Whit behind us.

made us feel more like tourists. It was a long, steep walk to the top, so our trusty guide provided a couple of donkeys to help us along the way. If that wasn't a picture; a group of GIs wearing stupid-looking tourist hats while riding jackasses up a mountainside on the Isle of Capri. From the looks of us, nobody could have guessed that crazy bunch of boys, just a few days before, had been flying treacherous combat missions in flak-filled skies.

Along the way, we ran into a B-24 crew and stopped to visit. It didn't take long to discover that their pilot was from Casper, Wyoming, Dunigan's home town. The two of them didn't know each other, but they knew some of the same people. The crew joined in with us and got in on riding the donkeys to the top.

Part of the crew at the castle ruins, L to R standing: the B-24 pilot from Dunigan's home town, McQuistion, Tucker in tourist hat, Garrison. Sitting in middle: Dwight, Sitting bottom: Whit and our guide.

Another adventure was taking a taxi up to

Anacapri, a little village at the top of a mountain. According to our tour guide, Anacapri was the setting for the song, *Isle of Capri.* About halfway up, we stopped at a little church, San Michelle, and went in for a look around. There, we all purchased a souvenir, *A Lucky Little Bell of San Michelle* - nobody needed luck more than us. The little bell had a chain attached that fit through a button hole on your lapel. Those bells were immediately attached to our uniforms and not removed until we got back to our base. Some of the guys flew their missions with that little bell in their pocket. I chose to leave mine under my bed safely tucked away in my make-shift foot locker along with my other souvenirs. My thinking was that if I didn't return, I wanted my family to have all my treasures. I managed to keep up with my lucky little bell and still have it today.

The church where we purchased our *Lucky Little Bell of San Michelle.*

An excursion to The Blue Grotto topped my list of all the places visited while on The Isle of Capri. The trip began at the harbor where we boarded small row boats, each manned by an Italian guide. The entrance to the cave was a small half-moon opening with a clearance of probably only about four feet. Patiently and skillfully, our guide waited for the perfect wave and maneuvered us into the cave on the trough of the wave. We had to lay down in the bottom of the boat to make the clearance.

The Blue Grotto

Once inside, it was like being in another world. The entire floor was a bright, shiny white which reflected off the walls of the cavern. That reflection caused the color of the water to be the most intense blue I've ever seen. The unusual phenomenon was caused by sunlight entering the cave through the underwater entrance. Once inside, our guide quietly paddled us around the grotto. The visitors were so amazed and spellbound by the unusual beauty that a hush fell over the place. Right away, I added the Blue Grotto to my list of places I would visit again someday; I haven't made it yet - but it's never too late.

One smart fisherman offered to take a few of us out for a little fishing trip, for a small fee, of course. I was curious to see how fishing was done in the Mediterranean, so I was anxious to go along. There were no poles, just some line wrapped around a stick. The fisherman baited the small hooks with shrimp he harvested with a fine-meshed dip net.

He caught about a half dozen fish that looked like our Spanish mackerel but only about ten inches long. We enjoyed the ride as he rowed us ashore where we said goodbye and he headed home with the fish. We got a big laugh out of the fact

Typical fishing and tour guide boats

that we paid him to take us out fishing so that he could catch his dinner.

After a few days, our new friend, the tour guide, suggested we visit Pompeii. Under his supervision, we took a boat back to the mainland and then a street car to the sight. It was obvious that he was very knowledgeable as he guided us through the ruins and told us the history of the eruption of Mount Vesuvius.

Our guide explained that in 76 AD Mount Vesuvius erupted, spewing lava and covering the city of Pompeii, killing thousands. Centuries later, archaeologists began unearthing the ruins and were very impressed by the sophisticated way the city had been constructed. Evidence was found of lead pipes used for plumbing and an intricate drainage system. Ruins were unearthed of grandeous bath houses with elaborate works of art on the walls.

Most of the surviving art work was visible to the public; however, there was some that was hidden from view. Our tour guide led us to a location where there was a frame built into the wall with a door attached. He motioned for us to move in close. When he was sure we were the only ones around, he took out a key and opened the door. We all just stood there and stared for a few seconds until somebody in the huddle let out a long whis-

A COMPANION TO THE VISIT OF POMPEII

BY AMEDEO MAIURI

(Director of the Excavations of Pompeii and Herculaneum)

POMPEI — TIP. FRANCESCO SICIGNANO — 1944

Cover of tour guide pamphlet that I saved as a souvenir.

tle and we all started snickering. The painting was of a Roman soldier all dressed up in his chest plate and helmet with laced up sandals - the whole works. He was standing in one of the bath houses with his fly opened. We got a full view of him holding a balance scale with gold bars on one side and his big ole tally whacker perched up on the other side. Our guide translated the caption: "Worth its weight in gold."

I always wanted to go back someday to see if the risqué paintings of life in Pompeii were still concealed behind locked doors. I would have been curious to see if tour guides still walked around the ruins with special keys to open the secret doors.

While in Pompeii, I bought a few souvenirs. One was a small bronze statue of Romulus and Remulus who were alleged to have founded Rome. The statue depicts the two young boys nursing from a she wolf. I also purchased a large colorful shawl that was weaved just like a fish net. The most expensive item was a beautiful cameo broach for my mother that I picked up at the little factory where they were made. My mom treasured the gift and often wore it to church and on special occasions. She kept it in a safe place in the back of her chiffarobe. My wife has it today.

Our guide took us to a real nice restaurant near Pompeii for a late lunch. When the waiter brought us a bottle of wine, the guide told him he would have to do better than that. In fact, our guide followed the waiter to the back of the restaurant where he talked to the manager. They all disappeared for a few minutes, and soon our guide returned with a bottle of wine in one hand and a huge grin on his face. They had been in the wine cellar searching for the perfect bottle. All I remember is the waiter had to wipe the dust off before he opened the bottle. It was absolutely delicious; I was certain that would be the best wine I would ever taste. We consumed several more bottles, though none quite as tasty as the first.

The week on The Isle of Capri certainly provided us with some much deserved rest and recuperation. For just a few days, we were able to escape the rigorous routine of flying combat. Though we hated to see the blissful week end, now we were even more motivated to get back, get our missions completed, and return home.

Mishaps, Malfunctions and Maladies

Chapter 29

Bombs

Everybody on the crew always felt relieved when we made it to the target and the bombs were dropped. Getting rid of those bombs lightened the load and the tension. On one mission, a 500 pounder didn't release from the top rack; consequently, it didn't fall with the others. Dunigan was going to drop it when we got over the Adriatic Sea, but a substitute bombardier advised Dunigan that it would be safe to land with the bomb. The guy said it was locked in, and he had taken the fuses out. Dunigan questioned him about his recommendation, but the bombardier was adamant that it was safe.

As usual, the gunners were all sitting around on the floor of the radio room when we came in for a landing. As soon as the wheels hit the ground...BANG! That bomb fell from the top rack, sprung the bomb-bay door open, hit the ground, bounced up, and knocked a giant dent in the underside of the plane. You should have seen the ground crew scatter when that bomb rolled across the runway and into a field.

With all the action going on outside the plane, inside the radio room the fuses from the stray bomb started bouncing around. We were all trying to grab them, that was, everybody except Michael. When those fuses started flying around, he headed for the back door like a rocket. He would have made it, too, if he hadn't hit the ball-turret support. Guess he would have jumped out with us going down the runway at 50 miles an hour. We teased him for the longest time because the cotter (safety) pins were still in the fuses.

As expected, just as soon as Dunigan landed the plane, he was all over the guy. That bombardier had to write a letter to the Commanding General of the 15th Air Force explaining the whole incident. I don't remember what happened to him, but I know he never flew with us again.

Another incident involving a hung bomb happened when we were carrying either 100 or 200 pound general-purpose bombs because our target was an airfield. After "bombs away," the radio operator looked and reported "one's hanging loose on the right side."

True to form, without hesitation, Dwight announced, "I'll take care of it." Before he could do anything, he had to disconnect from the oxygen supply and hook up to a walk-around bottle. He took his pliers out of his trusty canvas pouch, eased down and positioned one foot on the eighteen-inch cat-walk in the bomb bay and the other against the plane. He wasn't wearing a parachute because the chest pack would have been in the way. There was nothing under Dwight except about five miles to the ground. He grabbed the bomb, braced it against his leg, cut the wires loose, and let it fall. Then Dwight calmly climbed back to his position, hooked himself back up to oxygen, turned on the intercom, and started singing, *Take me back to Tulsa. I'm too young to marry*.

If Dwight hadn't been able to support that bomb, it could have fallen and hit the side of the bomb-bay door and exploded. He was awarded the Distinguished Flying Cross for his quick and heroic action. His bravery and loyalty may have won him the Cross, but for the guys on his crew it won him a special place in our memories that I, for one, still recall 65 years later. Clyde Dwight was truly one of a kind, and I was one fortunate young man to have been on his crew.

Once, lagging behind and having to drop a bomb to lighten the load actually paid off, big time. I can't remember the mission, but I do remember it was a long one. For some reason, on the way to the target, we began to lose power. Dunigan decided that we needed to lighten our load a little bit; so he told McQuistion, our bombardier, to drop one of the 500 pounders. Mac found the perfect spot in the snow and dropped the bomb into a small patch of forest, away from any populated areas.

The drop was a direct hit right into the middle of the forest. Instantly there was a huge explosion. No doubt, the forest had been a hiding place for oil-storage tanks. We weren't even halfway to the target and already we had made a direct hit. The explosion and fire was so great that some of the guys in the planes behind us reported seeing black smoke up to 20,000 feet. What a lucky drop!

I remember one other incident of lagging behind and having to drop bombs to lighten the load. We were almost to the target when we began to lose power and weren't able to keep up with the squadron. Dunigan ordered Mac to drop the first bomb and we almost caught up. Unfortunately, after a few minutes, we began to drop back again; Dunigan ordered another drop. That same procedure continued for quite a few drops.

In the meantime, the rest of the group completed the bomb run and was returning home. The leader of the fighter escorts radioed Dunigan and told him to turn around and join the returning group because there weren't enough fighters to protect a lone plane.

I never questioned Dunigan's decisions; when he declined and continued on, I figured he knew what he was doing. In no time, we were over the target and dropped our two remaining bombs: one 500 pound general purpose and one leaflet bomb. I think, because we were so close to the target, Dunigan wasn't willing to turn around. If he had, it would have cost us a mission count. If you don't drop your bombs over the target, you may as well have never taken off.

There was reason for concern, when one day, we were all called in for an unscheduled briefing. An intelligence officer informed us that there had been some suspicious activity indicating there might be German agents or Italians attempting to plant pressure-activated bombs in our planes. In the briefing, we were shown pictures of the suspect bomb which was about ten or twelve inches long and about an inch and a half in diameter. The bomb had a pressure-activated fuse that would set off at an altitude of about 10,000 feet. Because of its small size, it could have been easily hidden in our planes. There was no doubt it could do substantial damage or even bring down an aircraft.

For a short while, before every mission, crews had to scour every inch of their planes looking for a possible hidden bomb. We never found anything, but talk about nerves - what if we missed something? Everybody was real tense until we got up over 10,000 feet - like we didn't have enough to worry about.

For a brief time, one of the gunners had to sleep in the planes. There were security guards out on the flight line, but either they weren't trusted, or there weren't enough to provide adequate protection. The best I remember, I only slept in the plane once. Our down-filled sleeping bags kept us warm. You'd lay right there by the door of the aircraft with your Colt 45 real close by.

Nothing ever came of the whole incident, and soon we were back to our regular procedures. I think the precautions were justified because there had been documented cases of bombs being planted in the wheel wells of some B-24s in Italy. The story I got was that an American master sergeant on the ground crew was getting paid $1,000 for every bomb he planted.

Chapter 30

Parachutes

I would suspect that parachuting out of a plane over enemy territory would have to be right up toward the top of every flyer's list of fears. Not only did you face capture or death when you hit the ground, but there was also the fear of getting hit on the way down by German fighters or flak. For that reason, we were briefed not to open our chute until we were a safe distance below the flak.

I witnessed a jumper who almost died before he even cleared his airplane. We were in tight formation when a plane lower and to my left took a direct hit. I watched as the crew began to bail out. All went well until the last guy out pulled his rip cord just as soon as he stepped out of the plane. Immediately, the wind caught his chute and draped it over the tail of the plane where he dangled, helpless for a few seconds. No doubt, we both thought he was a goner. The sight took my breath away when, all of a sudden, that parachute peeled off the wing, feathered out, and opened up just as pretty as you please.

I made a mental note right then and there to make sure, if I ever had to bail, that I cleared the slip stream before I pulled my rip cord.

I had one experience with my parachute deploying, and it didn't happen jumping out of a plane. It was a typical mission, so when we approached enemy territory I began to make

my way back to the tail. As usual, I was pushing my chest-pack parachute in front of me as I crawled on the right side of the tail wheel to reach my position.

All of a sudden, and for no apparent reason, my chute deployed and immediately filled the tail end with nylon. Quickly, I gathered up the jumble and backed my way out. When I could stand up, I began stuffing the chute in my equipment bag as I tried to figure out what had happened. The culprit turned out to be a rivet pin that had been left sticking out by the sheet-metal guys when they repaired a flak hole. My rip cord caught on the pin as I was pushing the chute forward.

Enemy territory was rapidly approaching and so was oxygen altitude. I quickly reached for the spare parachute that was always kept on board. Unfortunately, it turned out to be a back-pack chute which, first of all, nobody liked and second, they were too bulky to take back in the tail. I asked, or maybe I even begged, both waist gunners to trade chutes with me, but neither would agree. Rather than give up his chest chute, Whit agreed to trade positions with me. That mission and my last mission were the only two times I flew anywhere but in the tail.

Chapter 31

Panic and Fear

We did have one incident of panic on board our plane. On that particular mission, our co-pilot, Garrison, was sick so we had a substitute, an inexperienced, rookie lieutenant. On our way up over the Alps, we experienced an oxygen leak. Dunigan and Dwight assessed the situation, determined the leak was minor, and decided to continue on. The nervous, rookie co-pilot did not agree with Dunigan and wanted to turn back. He put up quite an argument which was quickly dismissed.

As we approached the target, we got into some pretty heavy flak which was just too much for the lieutenant. He started begging Dunigan to turn back and started crying about his wife and two kids he wanted to see again. Dunigan chewed him out good and finally calmed him down. Later Dwight told us, "I had my hand on the fire extinguisher. If he hadn't calmed down, I was gonna bean him." He would have, too.

When we got back to the Alps, Dunigan told us all to sit down, not to move around, and breathe real light. Just as soon as we got over the Alps, he lowered the nose of the plane and got us down to 10,000 feet in record time. We were all mighty relieved when he gave us the all clear to take off our oxygen masks. Just to see how close we had come, I took one last breath through my mask and got a vacuum.

I will have to hand it to that rookie co-pilot though; later that afternoon he came by our tent and apologized to us all. It was obvious that he was embarrassed and very sorry for what he had done. I don't know if he apologized on his own or if Dunigan made him do it; regardless, he never flew with us again.

I never saw anybody lose their nerve and refuse to get in the plane; that wasn't an option. You got in the plane and prepared for the mission because that's what you had to do. Sure we were scared - so what?

Though I never witnessed anything but daily displays of bravery, I did hear of a couple of unfortunate incidents that happened before I got overseas. The first tale was about a young guy who did okay on his missions until the flak started. He wasn't afraid of flying; it was just that the flak was more than he could stand. On one particular mission, his crew was over the target and the flak got real rough. The story goes that the fella snapped his parachute on, walked over to the door, and bailed out. The story didn't conclude with what happened to him, but I kind of doubt if he survived. He probably got shot and killed before he hit the ground. If he did survive the jump and was taken prisoner and survived, he would have been court marshaled after the war was over.

Another story was about a guy who had only flown a few missions. His crew was loading up for a mission when he froze at the door. He told his crew that he just could not go through it again. He said he would rather die than get in that airplane. A crew member had to pry his fingers loose from the door and, ultimately, had to get another gunner to come out and take his place. He was taken to the flight surgeon who declared him incompetent to fly. He was allowed to stay on with the squadron, but he was reassigned to ground duty.

Switzerland, Turkey, and Sweden were neutral countries. If a plane went down in any of those countries, the flyers were interned for the remainder of the war. I have no firsthand accounts, but it was rumored that pilots were known to land in

one of those neutral countries even if they could have made it back to their bases.

Dunigan was appalled at such action; consequently, he assured us that he would never take us down in one of the neutral countries unless it was an absolute last resort. In fact, he asked us all to take an oath promising that if we should go down we would attempt to escape rather than be interned; the whole crew readily took the oath. It was common knowledge that American flyers were not treated very well in Switzerland because of the many German sympathizers in that country.

Memorable Missions

Chapter 32

Combat Mission #1

The day finally arrived, November 19, 1944, the first of my 35 required combat missions. If that wasn't stressful enough, I learned that first-combat missions were never flown with your own crew; instead, you flew with an experienced crew. I understood the logic, but it sure was a strange and scary feeling to board that Fortress and prepare for the mission with a bunch of strangers.

Rookie gunners were supposed to fly in either of the waist positions. That way you had a man standing opposite you to keep an eye on you. Nobody knows why, but I flew my first mission in the tail, and wouldn't you know - it was one of my roughest missions.

My biggest concern, on that first mission, was wondering if I was ready; was I really prepared for live combat? After giving it some thought, I decided that there was no way to be completely prepared. There was nothing more I could do except stay in my position, man my guns, and do what I was taught to protect the tail from enemy fighters.

The target was Munich. As we approached, the sky was full of 88mm flak bursts which were so thick, it didn't look like a plane could fly through it. After we were out of the flak, the pilot radioed me and asked me if I had seen any of our planes going down. I replied, "Sir, I was too busy watching for German fighters to notice." At any rate, the plane was bouncing around like crazy from the concussions of the flak bursts. There was nothing for me to do except hold on tight to my guns and keep my parachute real close by.

When we landed, the ground crew was right there to assess the damages. They surrounded the plane and began counting the holes to get an estimate of how long it would take to get her patched up. I remember one old master sergeant, walking around with his clipboard, reported there were 102 holes in the aircraft.

When I got back to my tent that afternoon, you might say, I was kind of dazed. The reality of what I had just been through began to set in. Before I had time to get my nerves settled, the operations sergeant came driving up and called me out to his jeep.

Much to my surprise, he explained the reason for his unexpected visit, "The crew chief said you got sick and puked in a helmet and left it in the plane."

"Like hell I did!"

To which he responded, "Well, since it was your first mission, they're all gonna blame it on you anyway. Tell you what I'll do; I'll take you back out there. You go in, get the helmet, and just throw the whole damn thing out behind the oil drums."

I did it, but I sure didn't want to. You can bet that, as I hurled that stinking helmet out of sight, I had a few choice words for the SOB who filled it. I just hoped I'd never fly with those guys again and couldn't wait to get back with my own crew.

Much discussion and debate went into how many missions would be required before a combat flyer had completed his tour of duty. Initially, 50 was the required number though that didn't mean 50 missions had to be flown. Flyers would be given credit for two missions if one was exceptionally long. By the time I arrived, 35 had been established as the required number. Every flyer was considered a "rookie" until they had flown at least five combat missions.

Chapter 33

Shot Down

It was Christmas Day of 1944 - my tenth mission. The Brux Oil Refinery in northern Czechoslovakia was a much-dreaded target because it was so far away. We had been scheduled there before, but each time we neared the target, bad weather moved in, and we had to hit an alternate target. But, on that particular Christmas Day, the weather conditions around the target area were excellent. Christmas Day, or not, we were scheduled to fly.

We flew past the target at about 28,000 feet. Our usual practice was to go up past the target and then come back down on it. As we were approaching, I called the ball-turret gunner and asked him, "Jack, what does it look like up front?"

"Tuck, it don't look good at all. It's gonna be impossible for a plane to fly through that stuff. It's so thick there's no way in the world we'll make it through."

"Don't tell me that Jack. It can't be all that bad."

Jack's reply was cause for concern, "You wait and see."

When we got even with the target, I could see quite a few parachutes. That was never a good sign. We continued on, turned and came back down on the target, and dropped our bombs. That's when we got hit. Immediately, the concussion caused the plane to shake violently. Dunigan lost control of the plane, and we started falling fast. I remember holding on for dear life and looking out the Plexiglas and seeing the sky whiz by. There was no doubt in my mind that we were done for. I clearly remember thinking, "This is it; our luck just ran out." Suddenly, the plane kind of leveled out. It took me a second or two to realize what was happening and to get myself together enough to, once again, man my guns.

I was able to hear a play-by-play through my earphones as Dunigan and Dwight struggled to assess the damages. One piece of flak had hit a push rod in the right-inboard engine and all the oil had spurted out. Dunigan just had time to feather it when we got hit with another piece. The second piece of flak hit the spinner, the hub of the prop, and shattered the feathering mechanism on the left-inboard engine. It just started wind milling, turning free. That engine was registering 3300 RPMs which was way more than the engine could handle. Now, we had a runaway prop which set up a drag.

Dunigan decided to try to shake the engine in hopes it would come out of its mount. Well, you can't shake a B-17 so that plan didn't work. Then he thought maybe the prop would work itself loose and come off - didn't happen. We kept losing altitude and air speed.

When we made it to the Adriatic Coast of Yugoslavia, Dunigan told us to prepare to ditch. The U.S. Navy had ships stationed in the Adriatic to pick up ditched crews. All the gunners assembled in the radio room with our parachutes hooked to our harnesses. All I remember thinking was, "Man, that water's gonna be cold." At first, Dunigan considered ditching; but the sea was so rough, he decided against it. He didn't like the looks of the terrain and decided it was too rough and ragged for us to jump. That was just fine with me. As a last resort, he made the decision to try to make it to the island of Vis.

The island of Vis is off the mainland of Yugoslavia. In the early stages of the war, Tito had escaped to the island when the Germans invaded Yugoslavia. American troops had taken over the island and set up a crude airfield there for crippled bombers that couldn't make it over the Adriatic Sea.

We made it to Vis "on a wing and a prayer" as the old saying goes. I think everybody was pretty happy to chance an emergency landing rather than face the freezing water of the Adriatic or the unknown of jumping. When Dunigan prepared to land, he had no hydraulics and no flaps. He didn't have time to go upwind and come up against the wind, so he had to make a downwind landing which was almost unheard of in a B-17. Dwight went back to the radio room, opened the floor hatch, and attempted to crank the flaps down. Before he could start cranking, the wheels touched down. There was no real landing strip to speak of, just some pretty rough terrain where there had once been a strip. It was a bumpy ride, but with every bump we knew we were on dry land.

As the plane slowed down, we noticed a small crowd had gathered. When we came to a stop, some members of the greeting party moved closer. We were all pretty anxious to get out of that plane, so I quickly opened the door. As long as I live, I will never forget those three women who were standing so close to the door they were actually blocking our exit. They were so scary, my first instinct was to slam the door shut and grab my pistol.

Each one of the women was about the size and shape of a refrigerator. Their uniforms looked like they were made out of those OD (olive drab) GI blankets. On their caps was the prominent Communist red star. Each one had a bandolier of ammunition with a sub-machine gun slung over their shoulders. Boy, they were mean looking, with no expression on their faces whatsoever. Those were the dangerous kind; with no expression, you didn't know what they were thinking.

They just stood there, glaring at us, until Dunigan came forward and attempted to get them to back up so we could get out. He wasn't having much luck, and I was beginning to think that maybe we should have ditched in the Adriatic. Thankfully, a Yugoslavian sergeant arrived, shooed the gigantic women aside, and greeted us. We quickly exited the plane and met our rescuer. He informed us that it was his responsibility to take care of any Allied crews who made emergency landings in the area.

To everyone's amazement, the sergeant spoke perfect English - I guess so, he was raised in Chicago. His family had moved to the United States when he was 12 years old and had returned to Yugoslavia for a visit. They became stranded when the war broke out, and he was drafted into the Yugoslavian Army. Because he spoke English, it was his job to look after all the Americans, British, and Australians who made emergency landings on Vis.

For whatever reason, the Yugoslavian sergeant made sure that we knew how much he hated the Germans. With pride, he lifted his pants legs and showed us all some pretty ugly scars. He explained that he had been cut down by German machine gun fire during a raid. He had received some serious wounds that took weeks to heal. Hopefully, he survived the war and made it safely back to Chicago.

We were soon joined by a B-24 crew who had been standing by watching us come in. They had scraped in just ahead of us. Their base was located south of us between Foggia and Cerignola. It was kind of interesting talking to the crew because none of us had ever spent any time around B-24s. The pilot was most impressed with Dunigan's emergency landing. Before we were all rescued, he got together with the rest of our officers and wrote up a citation for Dunigan to receive the Distinguished Flying Cross.

The Yugoslavian sergeant warned us to keep our distance from the local Partisans. He told us they were all beggars and thieves with particular interest in our pistols and our shoes. He warned us not to give them anything. From him, we learned that they were all illiterate mountain people. He didn't have to worry; none of us were interested in getting friendly with any of the locals.

It was common knowledge that a lot of planes went down on Vis, but there were no signs of any of them. There were no hangers or maintenance facilities that we could see. There didn't appear to be any kind of repair facilities. As suspected, we learned that the Yugoslavs dismantled every plane that went down and found some use for every part of the crippled planes.

We knew we would have to leave the *Kwitchubitchin* behind. There was no way she would ever fly again. It was sad to think of her being dismantled and her parts carted off to who knows where. Before I left to return home, the squadron received an unnamed plane which the ground crew quickly named *Kwitchubitchin II*. The best I remember, I never flew in her.

Dunigan was usually a step or two ahead of everybody. He had obviously noticed that we went down near a fishing village. "Tuck," he asked me, "since you were born and raised on the water, if we can't get anybody to come pick us up, could you get us across the Adriatic in one of those fishing boats?" I assured him that I could. I had noticed some pretty good size fishing boats and trawlers but had no idea that Dunigan was planning to commandeer one of them to get us home. I had to chuckle at the thought of me being the captain with Dunigan and the other officers being part of my crew.

Fortunately, it didn't come to that because we were able to get in touch with air rescue. They told us to sit tight - that was it - just sit tight; no idea about when or how they would pick us up. We were all relieved, beyond belief, to have been rescued by the Partisans, but we weren't too excited about the thought of sitting around with them not knowing when or how we would be rescued. We were anxious to get back to our base and continue with our missions.

Our Yugoslavian sergeant walked with us a short distance down a dirt road to show us where we could get some assistance from a group of American soldiers. There we found an American Army captain, eight enlisted men, a cook, and a bulldozer. The captain was an engineer who had been sent to the area to scrape out another emergency-landing field further up the coast. They had plenty of food and were happy to feed us that evening. We even had canned turkey for our Christmas dinner as we sat on the ground around their fire.

There wasn't much talk about it being Christmas; though, I'm sure everybody was thinking about home. I know, for my crew and the B-24 crew, we were all so thankful for the situation we were in. We had all escaped death, capture, and injury - what a Christmas present!

That night we slept upstairs in the hayloft of a barn. It was makeshift, no cots or any accommodations. We were given blankets, so we just hunkered down in the hay and tried to stay warm. I don't remember getting much sleep that night, probably because I was afraid that those three Partisan women, our greeting party, might be lurking somewhere in the dark.

The next morning, we had been invited back for breakfast by the American Army captain. When we arrived, the captain told us breakfast would be a little late. He explained that the cook had a Yugoslavian girlfriend that he shacked up with and he was always a little late. Sure enough, in a little while, he showed up and fixed us the usual powdered eggs and coffee.

In the meantime, we had another American flyer join us. He was a gunner who had bailed out somewhere near Vienna. For six weeks, the Partisans had helped him and had managed to smuggle him down to the coast. He had been brought over to Vis to wait for the next rescue pick up. It appeared that he had been well cared for; he looked healthy and was in good spirits. He sure was glad to see us.

We all jumped for joy when, shortly after breakfast, we spotted a Goonie Bird (C-47) approaching the landing strip. The pilot was making a drop of supplies for the Yugoslavian Partisans and had been told to expect some company on the way back. Talk about a happy bunch as we climbed aboard that big old bird. We were all taken back to our base where we said a hasty goodbye to the others. I couldn't wait to get a hot shower, get back to my warm tent and into my down sleeping bag for a much deserved good night's sleep.

On December 28th we were back flying combat missions.

Chapter 34

Purple Hearts and MIA

My twentieth mission, on February 1, 1945, was another of many to Vienna. Other than Berlin, Vienna was known to be one of the most heavily defended targets in Europe. Intelligence informed us that we could expect 360 antiaircraft guns at the target.

As expected, the flak that day was heavy, intense, and accurate. We reached the target, dropped our bombs, and had just turned off the bomb run when there was a flak burst right outside our plane, slightly behind me and to my left. Immediately, I felt the concussion and was slightly dazed from it. When my senses returned, I knew two things: my arm was burning, and the rudder cable had been cut.

Dunigan called, "Tuck, you okay back there?"

"Yea, I'm a little dazed, and my arm's burning pretty bad, but we've got other problems back here." I didn't want to alarm the rest of the crew about the rudder cable.

"Yea, I know." I heard him tell Garrison to have the first-aid kit ready and get the morphine out. "Get on up to the radio room so we can have a look at you. I'll send somebody back to relieve you."

I told Dunigan it could wait till we got out of flak and down to oxygen level. After a few minutes, I shed my flak vest and oxygen mask and made it to the radio room. Earl Whit was sent back to my position. The minute he got back there he called over the intercom, "Hey Dunigan, your rudder cable's shot loose!"

Garrison checked me over real good and found there was a small entry wound just below the shoulder of my right arm with a little blood trickling out. I knew, from the burning sensation deep in my arm, that I had been hit by a piece of shrapnel. Before long, Whit reappeared from the tail with my flak vest. He wanted to show us the huge rip in the canvas right in the middle of the back of my vest. Garrison and Whit concluded that I had taken a direct hit with a piece of flak about the size of a fist. Everybody had to take a look at the damage and marvel at the fact that I was still alive.

There was really nothing to be done, so I just sat on the floor in the radio room the rest of the mission. I was still pretty addled from the concussion and the realization that I had just had a close encounter with death. As I sat there, I began to feel soreness creep into the middle of my back. As the tenderness intensified, I couldn't help but imagine what that piece of flak would have done to my body if not for the protective vest. I could imagine the hot, molten metal ripping through my flesh and shattering my spine. That hideous thought stayed with me for days until the bruising and soreness left my back.

We were flying squadron lead that day, so Dunigan called the others and reported he would be making wide turns because he didn't have a rudder. Dwight went back to the tail to see what he could do. In his canvas tool bag, Dwight had short sections of cable and cable clamps. In no time at all, he called up and said the rudder cable was fixed; we proceeded on as if nothing had happened.

When we landed, Garrison signaled for one of the stand-by ambulances to follow us. I had told Dunigan that wasn't necessary and assured him I would get Doc Remley to take a look at my arm. Well, that wasn't good enough for Dunigan. He stopped at the end of the runway for me to jump out and hop into the waiting ambulance.

Doc Remley went in with a probe and tried to dig out the piece of shrapnel. Now, that was painful because he said he could feel it but just couldn't get a hold of it. Doc scanned the entry wound with a magnet and got no indication that it was metal, so he concluded that the fragment must have been a

piece of aluminum from the skin of the plane. Regardless, he decided to leave it in and told me it would probably work itself out. I felt it in my arm for the longest time. Eventually, I just forgot about it.

A few days after the incident, I was checking the bulletin board when one of the clerks called me into the office and told me he had my Purple Heart. He gave me a copy of my orders, reached in a box, and handed me my medal.

Today, all my medals from World War II are hanging on a wall in my daughter's home, along with a few photographs and souvenirs. She calls it my "Wall of Honor." I'll have to admit; I often pause before the display and marvel at how the years have passed. My attention always drifts to the old photographs of those brave young men. As I gaze at the faces of my crew, for a fleeting moment, those pictures seem to come alive and I can hear the faint sound of their laughter; sometimes, I think I hear them calling my name. As my eyes move from face to face, recalling each name, it's sad for me to acknowledge that they're all gone now, except for me. I'm the last one - the last voice - the only one left to tell our story. Sadly, I know that it's just a matter of time before I stand, for the last time, before my crew and make my *last roll call.*

Clyde Dwight, our flight engineer, also received a Purple Heart. I can't remember the mission, but I remember the incident very well. Our generator was located down behind the pilot's seat - down below the flight deck on the left-hand side of the cat walk. For some unknown reason, the generator shorted out and started smoking and blazed up. We had a bomb bay full of bombs, so something had to be done real fast. Dwight got down there with fire extinguishers but could never get the fire under control. By the time he emptied every fire extinguisher on board, he knew he had to do something drastic.

I was standing there watching when he reached down, grabbed the bundle of smoldering wires, and jerked them out. The fire burned through his glove and left his hand pretty badly burned. Once again, Dwight came to our rescue and, true to form, a bandaged hand barely slowed him down at all.

Unfortunately, that was a lost mission because we had no option but to return home. Because of the condition of the plane, Dunigan decided it would be too dangerous for us to land with the bombs on board. On the way back, Mac dropped the bomb load in the Adriatic Sea.

Because Halsey Nisula was such a great navigator, he was very much in demand and was often requested by the group-lead pilots. Toward the end of my tour, on one particular mission, we were all flying in the same group with Halsey in the group-lead plane. Dunigan and Garrison always kept an eye on the lead plane, and because Halsey was on board, they were paying even closer attention. You can imagine our horror when Dunigan reported the lead plane had been hit. He and Garrison had actually witnessed the hit and reported counting seven chutes getting out. Talk about an upset bunch of guys. We all thought the world of Halsey and felt so privileged to have him on our crew. That trip home was a sad one because all we could think about was that Halsey should have been with us. Halsey was reported as missing in action or captured. For the rest of my tour, we never heard anything; we just knew we had lost a good man.

Chapter 35

Other Targets

At briefing, one morning in March of '45, the operations officer pulled the screen down, "Gentlemen, today the target is Berlin." There was dead silence. "You heard me right, Berlin." You should have heard the groans and cussing; everybody knew we couldn't make it to Berlin.

When things quieted down, the officer attempted to ease our concerns by explaining that the weather people had reported that conditions were just right to make the long mission possible. The plan was for us to be over the target at 28,000 feet at exactly 14:30 hours which would put us in position to catch the forecasted tail winds back home.

We were further informed that our fuel tanks would be filled with every drop possible and our ammunition load had been cut in half. The operations officer suggested if there was anything on board we could do without to dump it.

Because of the long distance, even our fighter escorts had to do some coordinating to cover us. The P-38s escorted us to within 50 miles of Berlin. At that point, Squadrons of P-51s took over and furnished target cover. When we returned to the 50-mile rendezvous point, the P-51s headed home and were replaced by other Squadrons of P-38s. The fighter escort's coordination for the mission was outstanding.

As far as I know, the mission to Berlin was the longest the 15th Air Force ever flew. The Germans didn't think we could fly that far, so obviously we weren't expected. Consequently, it was reported that no alert was sounded until we were almost over the target. Even so, the flak gunners did manage to get off a few rounds from their towers. We were able to make a direct hit on the factory that produced Tiger Tanks for the German ground forces. Because the workers didn't have time to evacuate, it was reported that the raid killed or injured over 20,000 civilians. Supposedly, the wind storms created by the fiery infernos reached up to 70 miles an hour.

Unfortunately, on the trip home, several planes ran low on fuel and had to land in Russian territory. The Russians were known to be pretty good about returning crew members, but not so good at returning aircraft.

The mission to Berlin recorded the longest flight time on my record - 9 hrs. 20 min.

Some of the worst flak I remember was on a mission to Innsbruck, Austria, which was at the northern end of the Brenner Pass. It was an important rail yard and junction for the Germans. As we flew through the Pass, the anti-aircraft guns were positioned high up on mountainsides, so they didn't have far to shoot at us. Some of the guns were so close we could actually see the muzzle blasts. We were later told that we were in heavy, intense and accurate flak for 32 minutes. That was the longest amount of time we were ever pounded by flak.

We lost several planes that day, and the sky was full of parachutes. Nobody on our crew ever raised their voice or cussed on the intercom, but all of a sudden Michael let out a string of cussing like I had never heard. Dunigan immediately told him to hold it down. Michael responded, "Those #%^* Germans are shooting at those guys bailing out." Well, that got Dunigan's attention, and he told the rest of us to see if we could verify that.

When a pilot lowered his wheels, that was universally accepted as a sign of surrender. Bailing out was also a sign of surrender; that's probably why parachutes are white. We had heard occasional reports of Germans mowing down helpless men on their way down, and that day was no exception. The sight was just more than Michael could take. None of the rest

of us witnessed the atrocity, but I'm sure it was something Michael Joyce remembered for the rest of his life.

I flew five missions to Vienna, but one I particularly remember was when we flew a maneuver called "squadrons in trail." I know the whole Fifth Wing, and maybe more, went into the target one squadron at a time, dropping their bombs on the railroad-marshalling yards. It was estimated that there were bombs falling on the city for over two and a half hours. To make the affect even more terrifying, whistles had been placed on the bomb fins. The terror tactic was designed to rattle the nerves of the people of Vienna. The tactic rattled our nerves, too, because we were approaching the target one squadron at a time and not in close formation with other squadrons. Even though we were well escorted, approaching a target as a single squadron left you more vulnerable to fighter attack.

On one particular mission we were bombing the marshalling yards at Landshut, Germany. Because there were no flak guns, we were able to get in close at 13,000 feet. Just as the lead ship dropped their bombs, the pilot immediately radioed the rest of the group to hold their bombs; but it was too late. He reported that there were Red Cross emblems on top of many of the trains, but he hadn't seen them before he released his bombs. At that instant, one of the trains blew up which was followed by several explosions as others blew up. The Germans had disguised the trains loaded with ammunition as Red Cross.

Once, we bombed The Prague Air Drome in Czechoslovakia which was, among other things, a German fighter-pilot training school. Our fighter escort went in ahead of us and strafed the air field before we dropped our bombs. We were dropping fragmentation clusters which were six small bombs that were on one pod. When they were dropped, the pods came apart and the bombs scattered.

The German losses were high. Our fighters destroyed many German planes on the ground and some were shot down as they attempted to take off. When the fighters were through, we came in and finished them off. Altogether, it was reported the Germans lost 60 aircraft in that raid.

At least 13 of my 35 missions were to oil refineries such as Blechammer and Ruhland in Germany, Brux in Northern Czecholsovakia, and Moosbierbaum in Austria. The 15th was largely responsible for shortening the war by making it very difficult for the Germans to maintain enough fuel supplies. Toward the end of my tour, we began to see a decrease in the number of German fighters because they just didn't have enough fuel. *The Stars and Stripes* reported that the German Army was beginning to withdraw and was not able to mount any large offensives because of fuel shortage.

Chapter 36

Combat Mission #35

Because Dunigan was such a skilled pilot and in such great demand, he completed his missions before the rest of us. After he finished, Garrison moved over to the pilot seat, and I flew a few missions with him. On my last mission, unfortunately, I was assigned to a pretty green crew. It was April 23, 1945, and the mission was to Zezio in northern Italy. I flew left waist that day.

Understandably, guys were known to be real nervous on their last mission so it was customary for tail and ball-turret gunners to fly in a waist position so somebody could keep an eye on them. I'll have to admit, I was pretty jumpy. In fact, Doc Remley had noted on my medical records that I was showing slight anxiety on my last seven missions. Doc was real good about checking with the pilots to see how the crews were doing. Dunigan had talked with me and offered to request another rest camp for me. I assured him I'd be okay; I didn't want another rest camp - I wanted to go home.

Flying right waist, that eventful day, was a rookie gunner. On our way to the target, I couldn't believe it when I noticed him sitting on a leaflet box with his head leaning up against the side of the plane. He had his oxygen mask on and appeared to be asleep. I gave the box a swift kick, grabbed him, jerked him up, and told him to stand up. Before I had time to start chewing him out about the dangers of falling asleep on oxygen, I noticed that his gun wasn't loaded. We were approaching enemy territory and his ammunition belt wasn't across the

feedway. He took care of that in record time, and then I proceeded to chew him out royally. He was a corporal and I was a staff sergeant, but I would have done the same thing no matter what his rank. Remember, he was supposed to be keeping an eye on me.

The pilot was another case of inexperience and incompetence. He couldn't hold his position straight and the plane kept drifting back and forth. We were in a low group, and I soon noticed that he had positioned our left wing directly under the bomb-bay doors of the plane above us. I called the lieutenant and informed him of my concern.

"Oh, it's nothing to worry about. You're just nervous because it's your last mission," was his cocky response.

"You're darn right, but I've flown enough missions to know that bombs have been known to fall out of those bomb bays and hit the plane below it." He did move us over, but I could tell he wasn't the least bit concerned.

That was the worst disciplined crew I had ever had the misfortune of flying with. I never heard any communication between the officers and any of the crew. Man, I sure did miss my crew that day. We stayed in constant touch with each other. If you saw anything, you reported it; if you thought of a joke, you shared it with everybody.

No words can tell you how I felt when the bomb run was over and we were out of enemy territory and on our way home. I remember thinking surely this bunch of losers won't mess up before we make it home. It was a mighty powerful feeling to climb down out of that B-17 and set foot on the ground, knowing that I had just completed my 35th, and last, combat mission.

After briefing and chow, I took a shower, changed clothes, and went on down to the club. The custom was that the crew finishing up their missions would buy the bar out. Since I was the only one finishing up, I wanted to make sure there was plenty to drink before the rest of my crew and everybody else got there to celebrate. On occasion, the bar would sell out, and we just did without until another shipment arrived. When the

bar keep informed me he was out of stock, I told him that just wouldn't do and explained that I had just completed my last mission. He quickly reconsidered, "No sweat," he reassured me and sent one of his guys down the road to another outfit to resupply.

In a little while I went back and, sure enough, there was plenty of booze and the bar was full. But, instead of me buying drinks for everybody, they all bought drinks for me. I proceeded to sit there and get plastered. That was the first and last time, I guess, that I had been completely inebriated. Everybody was encouraging me because they kept saying, "Boy you got it made now. You're going home!"

Before I got completely plastered, Earl Whit said he had to talk to me about something real important. I knew something was up because he had a real serious look on his face which was completely out of character for him. We had taken a liking to each other when he joined our crew as our permanent left-waist gunner. We had gotten to be buddies as we palled around together at rest camp. I couldn't imagine what was troubling him.

Earl hung his head as he confessed, "Tuck, remember your first mission?" He hesitated as I shook my head.

"Remember, it was a real rough one? I had only flown a couple of missions myself and I was still pretty green. So, when I got sick and filled my helmet, I hid it; I didn't want anybody to know it was me. You were the new guy, the rookie. I knew they'd all think it was you; and besides, I never thought I'd see you again. Tuck, I sure am sorry. I just couldn't let you go home without telling you."

I was so happy about just completing my last mission that nothing, and I mean nothing, could have upset me - I was going home.

Needless to say, when I finally did wake up about noon the next day I was feeling pretty rotten. Even as hungover as I was, I managed to feel the joy of knowing my days of combat flying were over. Even through my blinding headache and nausea, I took comfort in knowing that I was going home.

I managed to get up, go to the chow hall, and stop by the Orderly Room to check on my orders home. That's when I ran into Doc Remley. He took one look at me and suggested I spend a few days at the rest camp in Rome before I headed home. "Ace, you don't want your family to see you in the shape you're in." I didn't have the heart to tell Doc that I was just suffering from the worst hangover I had ever experienced.

I declined the offer to Rome. "Doc, I'll be alright. I just want to go home. I don't care anything about seeing Rome; I've seen all of Italy I ever want to see." If I passed up rest camp, I figured surely I'd get home quicker. My sister, Thelma, had written reminding me that she would be graduating on June 6, and she sure hoped I'd be home in time to attend.

Headed Home

Chapter 37

Naples

Doc Remley gave in and sent me on to Naples on May 2, 1945. Our accommodations were in buildings constructed by the Italian government for a pending World's Fair. What irony - cancelling a World's Fair for a World's War.

Seems like we hung around the staging area for weeks. There was nothing to do and absolutely no where to go. I did send my last V-mail telling my family I would be on my way home soon. I know that was one letter they were proud to receive.

On May 8, 1945, we heard on the radio that the Germans had surrendered. Sure, we were all expecting it but to have it happen while I was still in Europe was pretty significant to me. I remember some celebrating with horns blowing, bells ringing and shots being fired to commemorate Victory in Europe.

True to military procedures, there were duty officers running around with clipboards trying to round up guys for details. They might have rounded up a few guys but not my roommates and me. Whenever we heard a knock on the room next door, followed by voices out in the hall, we would jump the two or three feet to the balcony of that room. We would wait there until the sergeant decided we were out. I don't know what they did other than pull KP, and luckily I never had to find out.

I remember one incident when I overheard some inspecting general questioning a master sergeant. "What did you do today sergeant?"

"Nothing, Sir."

"What did you do yesterday?"

"Pulled KP, Sir."

"You mean to tell me they've got master sergeants pulling KP. That's unheard of. NCO's won't be pulling KP around here anymore!" Little did the general know the guy probably volunteered just to have something to do.

I turned 20 on May 21, 1945, while waiting around in Naples. I don't think I even mentioned it to anyone. There were no birthday cards that time because my family knew I would be in transition; we would celebrate my birthday when I got home.

Shortly before we left Naples, there was a knock at our door. It was late in the day so we didn't suspect a duty officer. When I opened the door, I got a great surprise; it was Jack Taylor, our ball-turret gunner.

"Hey Tuck! Thought you'd get home before me didn't you? Well I fooled you. Man, I still had two missions left, but it's over - we're all going home."

The afternoon before we sailed, we were ordered to report to a conference room and bring all of our photographs, diaries, and anything else along that we intended to take home with us. I'm not sure who made the rules on what passed censorship and what didn't. I think it just depended on who was doing the checking that day. Regardless, my diary was confiscated because, they said, I had too many specific details about missions. The floor around the checker's desks was littered with confiscated photographs.

After that, we were ordered to report to the rooftop with all our belongings for a shakedown inspection. There, we had to strip down to our skivvies, then unpack our bags and lay out every single item for inspection. I don't know what they were looking for but, whatever it was, I didn't have any.

Early the next day, we were loaded on six-by trucks and hauled down to the pier. There, we were put into groups and ordered to wait until we were called to board. The longer I waited, the hungrier I got. By the time my group was finally called to board ship, it was 15:00 hours.

My group was marched down toward the end of the pier where one of those stream-lined cruise ships was docked. My spirits quickly lifted at the thought of sailing home on one of those sleek, fast, luxury liners. Just as we were about to approach the liner, I heard "Left turn!" We marched down a narrow pier where we were greeted by an old, rusty liberty ship.

Chapter 38

The Liberty Ship: *SS Lyman Abbott*

As I walked across that gang plank, my disappointment was about to overtake me when I remembered, "I'm going home. If I have to get there on this rusty old tub, then so be it." Conditions inside the ship were pretty rough, too, but I made the best of it. The realization that I had survived the war in one piece, and was headed home, was all it took to keep me upbeat and content the entire trip.

We didn't get on board until late that afternoon. There had been no lunch, and by now it was supper time. I was hot, tired, hungry and anxiously awaiting a decent meal. As we boarded, to my disappointment, we were each handed a K-ration and told the kitchen would be up and running in the morning. The miserable expression on my face caught the attention of one of the ship's crew members, a Merchant Marine. The guy had just finished up his supper and was headed back to his bunk with a big ole thick, pretty sausage sandwich in his hand. He took one look at my face and handed the sandwich to me. "You look like you need this worse than me." Oh boy, was it good - I shared it with the guys on either side of me.

We were in the Mediterranean for three days. From Naples we sailed to Oran, Algeria. There, we were delayed overnight while we waited for the remaining 20 ships that would make up our convoy. Even though the war in Europe had ended, a destroyer escort was ordered because quite a few German subs were not accounted for.

For three days, several American Navy blimps followed us out into the Atlantic. Two or three at a time patrolled the area around the convoy looking for enemy submarines. The trip across the Atlantic to Hampton Roads, Virginia, took 17 days.

All total, I spent 20 nights on that old liberty ship but only the first night down in the hold where I was assigned a bunk. There were an untold number of troops crammed together in four holds. The canvas bunks were stacked four high and so close together you bumped the guy above you when you turned over. Claustrophobia was something I had very little trouble with back in the crowded tail of a B-17, but being packed in with all those bodies was just too much for me. There was little ventilation, so you can imagine the smell. I couldn't breathe, much less sleep, with all the snoring, farting, and coughing going on.

The next day Jack, me, and a couple other buddies did a recon of the deck and found a perfect spot to make a camp for the rest of the journey. In between some pieces of equipment, piles of life jackets were covered up with tarpaulins. We took one of the tarpaulins, strapped it between the tops of the equipment, and spread the life jackets out under it. At night, we'd fold the tarp back and fall asleep gazing at the stars. The fresh ocean breeze and the steady hum of the engines sure made for some comfortable nights - what luxury.

We were fed twice a day, which was adequate, because nobody was doing anything to build up much of an appetite. The food wasn't too bad; there just wasn't much of it. I do remember a time or two asking for seconds and being refused. After one particularly slim dinner, Jack and I decided to pay a visit to the kitchen to see if we could find any leftovers. All we managed to find were several large, unmarked cans, so we helped ourselves to a couple. Turned out they were apricots which we quickly consumed until our stomachs were full - to this day, I'm not fond of apricots.

I didn't have any trouble keeping my rations down, but some poor guys suffered from seasickness the entire trip. There were a few guys who just about wasted away because as soon as they tried to eat, they would be yodeling over the side. The weather was just about perfect with smooth seas most of the way and just occasional gentle swells. I figured the guys who stayed sick had to be infantry or ground crews who were not used to the continuous motion.

As far as I know, the only officers on board were a doctor and a chaplain. They bunked up on top with the ship's officers. We were fortunate to have a doctor on board because one of the soldiers developed appendicitis. Because there were no operating facilities on board, a Navy destroyer in our convoy came alongside probably about 20 yards from us. The sailors fired a line to our ship which had a pulley system attached. Suspended from the pulley was a breeches buoy which looked like a round-life preserver with a piece of heavy canvas attached with two holes cut for the person's legs to fit through. First, the sick guy was loaded into the buoy and pulled over to the destroyer, then the apparatus was sent back to pick up the doctor. The whole exchange took less than an hour, but it provided some quality entertainment for a ship load of bored soldiers.

You could take a shower anytime you wanted if you didn't mind showering in salt water from the Atlantic Ocean. Well, I minded and so did lots of others. I never remembered feeling so sticky after swimming in the Gulf. Fortunately, there were a few rain showers along the way; so you can imagine how some of us crowded the deck, stripped down to our skivvies, and enjoyed the only source of fresh-water showers we had. The crew told us they would turn the fresh water on before we got to port so everybody could have at least one fresh-water shower before going ashore.

There was no formal entertainment of any kind. We were left to our own devices to pass the time. Once or twice, we were rationed one beer each. They were hot, of course, but they sure made for a nice change. I tried my best to talk some of my buddies out of theirs, with no luck.

At the beginning of the voyage, one old Merchant Seaman told us he'd have us some pretty good tasting wine before we reached port. He invited some of us down into the engine room to show us where he made his "Raisin Jack."

Down below, where it was nice and warm, he had some government-issue raisins and prunes fermenting in a stone crock.

He was a crusty old fellow who had his social security number tattooed to the underside of his right arm. He explained that no matter how drunk he got, if he could make it back to his ship and show his social security number, they would let him back on board.

His career in the Merchant Marines began, he explained, when he came home early one day and caught his wife in bed with the preacher. He said he turned, walked out the door, and headed to the first port he could find and signed up. His job was that of a wiper, the lowest position on the ship. He walked around the engine room with a rag and wiped up any oil spills or drips.

As promised, a few days before we landed, he proudly invited a few of us down to try out his "Raisin Jack." First of all, it smelled awful, and tasted even worse. A few guys managed to down a few sips; but mostly, the old drunk had his "Raisin Jack" all to himself. I kind of think that's the way he planned it.

Boredom made us do some stupid things. One of the most ridiculous was a little trick we pulled called, "forming a line." For lack of anything better to do, three or four of us would get together and stand in front of a door. Pretty soon two or three others joined our line; before long the end of the line would be out of sight. When guys had absolutely nothing to do, guess they figured they may as well go ahead and get in line even if they didn't know what it was for.

Books were very scarce and in great demand by those of us who enjoyed reading. We worked out a real unique system to share our books. A group of us would sit down in a line on the edge of the forward hatch. The first person in line, usually the owner of the book, would begin by reading the first page, then tear it out and pass it to the next person. The pages were passed down the line until they reached the last person who would stack all the pages in order so that somebody could pick up from there.

What a sight that must have been; sometimes two, sometimes ten guys, all with their heads buried in the pages of one book. Sure, we lost a few pages to the wind and there were a couple of slow readers who held up the line a bit, but we didn't care. It helped pass the time, and besides, soon there would be plenty of books to read.

When there wasn't a book to read, or a line to start, one of my favorite pastimes was standing up on the bow watching the flying fish and porpoises. The porpoises seemed to know they were in convoy heaven with so many wakes to ride and so many people watching. They entertained us the whole trip home.

There was one continuous crap game from the day we boarded the ship until the day we docked. One guy ran the show. He had even lined the dice table with a GI blanket. He ran that dice table night and day with onc helpcr who took over for him to go the bathroom, eat, and sleep. Whenever I went down to get something out of my duffle bags, I would hang around and get caught up in the excitement for a few minutes, but I never participated.

Up on the deck, we had little dime poker games going; mostly we played stud. When I got on board ship, I counted my money, and when I got off the ship I counted it again. I left the ship with $4.50 more than when I got on; obviously, I had some luck with the cards.

Pretty soon after we got on board, somebody came around and collected a dollar from everybody who wanted to get in on a pool to guess the exact day and hour we would sight the USA. As we got closer and closer to the United States, guys began to congregate on the bow, especially the infantry soldiers. Some of those guys had been overseas for three years and were very anxious to get the first glimpse of their homeland. Others were there to witness the day and hour of the first sighting of land to see who would win the pool.

Before reaching land, the convoy split up with ships headed to ports all along the Atlantic Coast. An excitement you just can't imagine filled that old liberty ship when those tug boats pushed us up to the dock at Hampton Roads, Virginia. There was even a band there to greet us. Whatever they were playing didn't sit well with the infantry guys because they kept chanting, "Robin Hood, Robin Hood." I'd never heard of the song, but the chanting persisted until they drowned out the band.

I got the biggest kick out of watching those infantry soldiers walk the gang plank to American soil. They managed to be first off as some of them victoriously waved Nazi battle flags. Many of them proudly displayed German helmets and German Luger pistols. Remember, we were searched in Naples and had to give up almost all our souvenirs. Obviously, nobody bothered to search the infantry soldiers - or maybe nobody dared.

The festivities at the port went on for quite awhile with guys hugging, back slapping, and kissing the ground. The relief of finally getting home was just too much for a couple of guys who sat down on the ground and cried. I was caught up in the excitement and loving every minute of it.

Chapter 39

Welcome Home

The excitement continued as we journeyed to Camp Patrick Henry, Virginia, where we were treated to a meal of steak with all the trimmings. The one thing everybody missed the most, fresh milk, was plentiful and, to make it even better, it was freezing cold. I gulped down as much milk as I could hold, and when I couldn't hold any more, I would just hold the freezing liquid in my mouth. I still love milk to this day, but it has to be freezing cold.

Everybody was caught up in our excitement and happiness. Even the German POWs, who were serving us dinner, were happy. They were laughing and cutting up and seemed to be enjoying serving us. I guess so; they knew that soon they would be returning home, just like us.

The next morning after breakfast, with plenty of cold milk and real eggs, we all disbursed on trains headed in all directions. My train took me to Fort McPherson near Atlanta. Because it was a troop train, the excitement continued all the way to Atlanta.

I was held over a day or so at Fort McPherson. While there, I ran into a guy I went to high school with, Lelman Taylor. When I shook his hand, I could tell he was green; something about the way their uniforms fit always gave them away. When I asked him how long he'd been in, he replied, "Three days."

In Atlanta, I boarded a Trailways bus for the final leg of my journey home. Several soldiers were on board with me as we traveled to Tallahassee. When I changed busses in Tallahassee, I picked a window seat on the driver's side so I would have a direct view of the bay when we reached the coast. As the bus pulled away, I looked around and realized that, for the first time in over two years, I wasn't surrounded by soldiers. It was just me; I was the only soldier onboard. That's when I also realized that the greatest adventure of my lifetime was ending just the way it began - on a Trailways bus.

You can only imagine the excitement I felt when the bus rounded a curve near Lanark and I caught my first glimpse of the water. The coastline greeted me like an old friend, a friendship that would soon be rekindled. As the journey continued, the highway weaved away from the coast and back again. With every sighting of the coast, I knew I was getting closer to home.

I took in all the sights as the bus passed through Carrabelle, and I recalled many of the same thoughts I had as I passed through over a year ago. I remembered the excitement of knowing I was about to embark on a once in a life time adventure but not knowing to where. Now, the adventure was complete; history had been made, and I had been part of it. But again, I was facing the unknown; this time not knowing where my life as a civilian was going to take me.

When the bus rounded the curve at Green Point, off in the distance, I could see the few seafood houses that lined the shore of East Point. There was no staying seated after that. With my musette bag slung over my shoulder, I stood on the steps as I cautioned the driver that he was about to make an unscheduled stop. My family had moved into a little house up on Hwy. 98 to be closer to Dad's business.

Through the front window, I saw my dad jump up off the steps of the crab house and run toward the bus. When the bus stopped and I stepped out, my dad had almost reached me. He was running from the crab house hollering, "Kenneth's home! Kenneth's home!"

When my dad grabbed me, I could feel his body shake with relief. I remember the smell of cooking crabs on his skin and clothes; for once, I rejoiced in that smell. When he finally let me go and I could look at his face, tears were in his eyes - he looked older.

Over Dad's shoulder, I saw my mom and two youngest sisters, Dattie and Loyce, running up toward the highway. My mom reached me first and just kind of fell into my arms and buried her face in my chest. I remember that she smelled like fried fish and Clorox. When she finally raised her head and I was able to look at her face, I was startled to notice, for the first time in my life, just how strong my mother's Italian features were.

My sisters, Dattie and Loyce, were jumping around like monkeys. I picked them both up at once and twirled them around as they each hugged my neck. They both smelled like trouble. When I finally had a look at them, I couldn't believe how grown up they were.

In the midst of the happy moment, I noticed that the bus hadn't pulled away. I looked up to see grinning passengers hanging out the opened windows as they watched my homecoming. Through the open door, the driver was also watching the joyful reunion. I was happy to share that special moment with those strangers; but in spite of all the joy, for just a fleeting moment, I sadly thought of all the families who would not be experiencing a homecoming with their loved one.

Eventually, the bus pulled away, and we moved into the yard and toward the house. My sisters were both talking at once and hanging on either side of me, making it difficult to walk. By now, my brother, Arthur, had made his way from the crab house to greet me. He looked so much older and so mature. They all said I looked older, too - they just didn't know the half of it.

Finally, we made it into the house where dinner was waiting. Before we ate, I changed into civilian clothes; that was a shock. I remember looking down at those strange clothes hanging on my body and wondering if I knew how to be a civilian again.

I remember my mother's face as she buzzed around the table making sure everybody had their fill of fried mullet, lima beans, and coleslaw. Her face beamed with joy and relief, and every time she passed me, she squeezed my shoulder. After dinner there was birthday cake. It sure was nice to be celebrating with family. My oldest sister, Hilda, had married one of the soldiers from Camp Gordon Johnson in Carrabelle and moved away. Thelma had moved to Jacksonville to attend business school as soon as she graduated - I sure did miss them.

We all stayed up late that night. It was difficult to give in and go to bed, but everybody had to work the next day, and I was weary from many days of traveling. As I lay in bed that night with the familiar breeze blowing off the bay, my last thought before falling asleep was, "I'm home."

For 30 days, I relaxed and enjoyed my family and friends. At first, my nerves were pretty frazzled, and I was real jumpy. My mom tried to keep everybody quiet, but that was next to impossible with six people in one little house. Every time the screen door slammed, I jumped like it had been a flak burst. I do know that my nerves have never been the same since flying combat. To this day, loud sudden noises still make me jump. What's frightening is the fact that the older I get, the jumpier I get.

For awhile, I had trouble sleeping. I'm not sure why except maybe I just couldn't get out of combat mode; maybe my body still needed the stress and anxiety of flying combat to shut down and sleep. I might not have slept much at first, but at least I never had combat-related nightmares; although, I do recall having a couple of bad dreams about those three Partisan women who greeted us at the door when we made the emergency landing on Vis.

In an attempt to try to calm my troubled nerves, I often headed to the one place I knew I would find peace and strength - our old home place. The familiar surroundings seemed to take me back to my childhood, before war and loneliness and death.

Every day as I walked the beach of my youth, the innocence of my childhood seemed to seep back into my body and quiet my frazzled nerves. Sometimes, I would lay on the pine straw and breathe in the faint smell of turpentine as I watched the tops of the tall pines gently sway. The soft rustle of a breeze high up in the top of the pines seemed to soothe my weary soul.

I spent a lot of time over at the crab house with Dad and Arthur. We could get away from the women folk and talk about the war. Now, I had joined the ranks of war veterans, like my dad. How strange it seemed to talk about the war from my personal experiences. I shared experiences with Dad and Arthur that I didn't care to talk about with other people. I was warmly greeted by the local fishermen who still mended their nets and repaired their boats on the beach next to the crab house. They wanted to know all about my experiences and never seemed to tire of my stories.

Dad and I enjoyed making the usual runs to Apalachicola. Now, I wasn't so interested in war talk or history lessons. I just stuck with my dad as we made our usual rounds. On one trip I did pay a visit to Sangaree's Barbershop for a haircut. I spoke to everybody as I walked in and had a seat in one of the barber's chairs. As he draped the towel over my shoulders, Vito Sangaree inquired, "Aren't you that Tucker boy from East Point? Hear tell you been flying fighters in Europe."

I corrected him, "Yea, I just got home. I wasn't a fighter pilot though. I was a B-17 tail gunner with the 15th Air Force out of Italy."

"Well, that's even better. What was it like back there in the tail?"

After a few days of staying close to home and spending time with family, I felt the need to venture out a little; besides, I had money to spend. Every month I sent money home to my dad for safe keeping and had managed to accumulate over $900. Back then, that was a lot of money. Arthur had a car and was always ready to chauffeur me anywhere I wanted to go.

There were a couple of girls I wanted to look up. The one in Panama City had been a friend of mine from high school and had written to me the whole time I was overseas. Arthur took me over, and we all had a great time with her and some of her girlfriends. We went out to Panama City Beach and built a huge bonfire. I actually made quite a few trips to Panama City while I was home on leave. On one trip, Arthur and I stopped by the Tally-Ho to check out the car hops - nobody looked interesting.

Another girl lived in Sopchoppy; she had been a friend of one of my sisters. I met her just before I left, and she and I had taken a liking to each other. She was real good about writing; consequently, we got to know each other through letters. I was anxious to get to know her in person, so I made a few trips to visit her in Sopchoppy, and she came and visited me a time or two. We had a great time because she knew my sisters and fit right in with the rest of the family.

My lifelong friend, Oma Boyington, was also home on leave. He and I traveled to Tallahassee once or twice to meet up with a couple of girls at Florida State College for Women (later to become FSU). He had been dating one of the girls and took me along to meet her roommate. We all hit it off and had a great time in the big city.

During my time at home, I received a letter from Cille, the party girl I met in Fargo while at Morehead for Cadet Training. Shortly after I arrived in Italy, she had written to my family asking for my address. Even though she only knew my family name and hometown, they received her letter. We wrote the rest of the time I was overseas and she and my oldest sister, Hilda, wrote for awhile. In the most recent letter, she asked me to meet her in Chicago after I was discharged. I wrote back and told her that was about the dumbest thing I had ever heard of.

During my leave time, I played a little tennis down at the Browns. I remember thinking how strange it was that the last time I played had been on the Isle of Capri. There were also the beach parties at Lagoon Beach, a trip or two over to St. George Island, and the movies at the Dixie in Apalach. I did some gill netting and duck hunting with my dad, uncles, and cousins. Mom and the girls and me made a trip or two up to Cash Creek and Whisky George Creek and caught a few bream. At the end of those 30 days, surprisingly, my life was getting back to normal.

After 30 days at home, I put my uniform back on and again boarded a bus for a long, hot ride to Miami Beach for a week of rest camp. Like Capri, most of the hotels had been leased by the Armed Forces. My accommodations were great at the President Madison Hotel. All of Miami Beach was crawling with returning soldiers, so everybody was in great spirits. Like me, their tour of duty was over and most would soon be home for good.

I was very fortunate to meet up with Clyde Dwight, our flight engineer, and his wife. It was great to see him and reminisce about old times. It was funny how we seemed to only recollect the funny and exciting times. The horror of war was behind us, and that's the way we wanted to keep it. I bragged to his wife about how resourceful her husband was and how lucky we were to have him on our crew. Because they had a car, we were able to venture out and see more of Miami Beach. Customary to Dwight's personality, he acted as tour guide and showed us a great time.

Postcard of the President Madison Hotel.
Written on the back, "This is where Oma (Boyington) and I are living now."

Also, my friend from home, Oma Boyington, was there at The President Madison. Like me, he had just finished his 30 days at home after returning from the Pacific where he had flown combat as a flight engineer on a B-25. It was great to have someone from home to pal around with.

The week passed quickly, and I was soon on a train headed for Ellington Field near Houston, Texas. While at Ellington, I was assigned to an administrative squadron and, from there, I was assigned to a position in the Post Office where, for about three months, I worked as a postal clerk.

Houston was a great town, and I sure had some good times there. Because there was so much to do, my buddies and I spent most of our free time in the big city. There were some nice dance halls where we had pretty good luck with the ladies. I wasn't much of a dancer, but I enjoyed the big band music. I did meet one girl that I liked and we dated for awhile. She got a little too serious, though, and started calling me at the post office. The last time she called, I told my buddy to tell her I had volunteered for another tour as a gunner in the Pacific and had been transferred to Las Vegas.

Once again, I met up with Jack Taylor, the ball-turret gunner. Immediately, I knew something was troubling him. "Tuck, your letter from Dunigan is probably waiting for you at home. Dunigan wanted to let us all know that he had heard from Halsey's family. His family reported that they had received a message from The Red Cross. Halsey had parachuted out safely but had been taken prisoner. The Red Cross reported that he had been shot and killed in an escape attempt."

The news was a real blow to me because we all held out hope that Halsey could have survived the war in a POW camp. He, like so many others, was such a great guy and so skilled at what he did - what a loss. I thought of Halsey's family and all the other families who had lost loved ones in the war, families who would never have the opportunity to cross the ocean and visit the final resting place of their loved one. I could only imagine how the families must have grieved even more at the thought

of their soldier being left behind, all alone and so far away. But, I had to think that they weren't alone; they had plenty of company, thousands of other brave, young men just like themselves.

I also learned, from Jack, that I should have taken Doc Remley up on his offer to go to rest camp in Rome before heading home. Jack informed me that all the guys who opted for rest camp before returning to the states were flown home. What can I say? You win some and you lose some. Oh well, at least because of my bad choice, I had my stories to tell about the *SS Lyman Abbott*.

While in Houston, Japan surrendered and the war was over in the Pacific. There was a huge parade in downtown Houston where folks crowded the streets to celebrate. Most of the squadrons from the base marched in the parade, and we received a tremendous reception. It was fun to march with real bands and a crowd of cheering civilian spectators. I noticed lots of pretty girls waving, and I had a great time waving back.

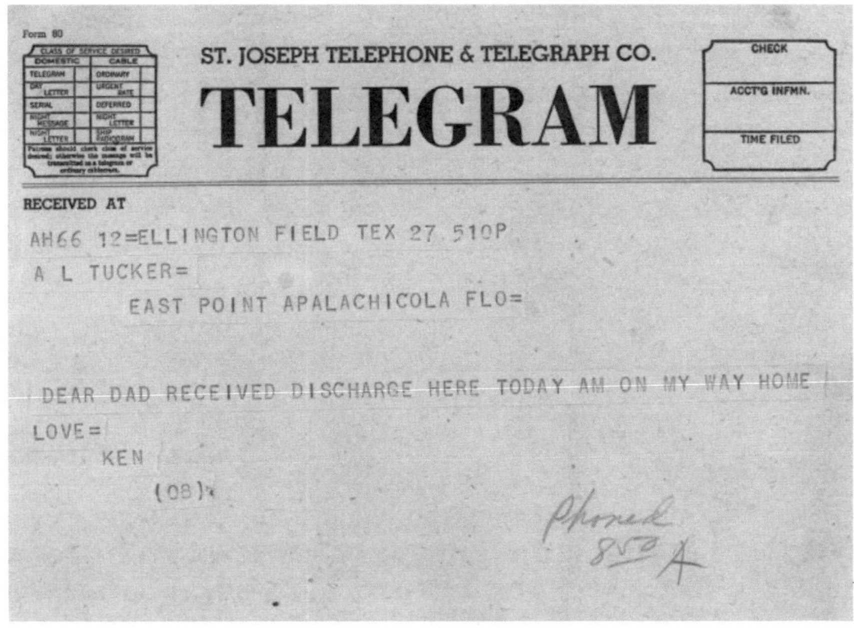

Form 80

ST. JOSEPH TELEPHONE & TELEGRAPH CO.

TELEGRAM

CHECK

ACCT'G INFMN.

TIME FILED

RECEIVED AT

AH66 12=ELLINGTON FIELD TEX 27 510P

A L TUCKER=

EAST POINT APALACHICOLA FLO=

DEAR DAD RECEIVED DISCHARGE HERE TODAY AM ON MY WAY HOME

LOVE=

KEN

(08)

Phoned 850 A

Telegram reads: "DEAR DAD RECEIVED DISCHARGE HERE TODAY. AM ON MY WAY HOME. LOVE KEN.

After three months, I was discharged. As expected, there was no fanfare of any kind. A clerk handed me my discharge papers, and soon I was on a bus headed home.

When I was almost home, the bus made a stop at Tyndall Army-Air Field near Panama City to drop off some passengers. I was sitting right behind the driver when, as one fella started to get off, he stopped, looked at me and asked, "Weren't you on Dunigan's crew?"

Of course, I was shocked and it took me a minute to remember the guy, but when he told me he was Sgt. Groney, I did recognize him. It was great to talk to him, especially since he remembered everybody on my crew. I was sad to have to tell him about Halsey.

The bus driver seemed to be interested in our conversation and told us to take our time. So, we talked for a few minutes before he stepped off the bus, and I continued on my journey home.

On that last bus ride home, my thoughts were about my future. I had my 30 days leave at home to relax, have fun, and enjoy my friends and family. Now, it was time to get serious. There were no jobs to speak of in Franklin County. I knew that at home my only option would to be to work in the seafood business.

By now, Arthur was helping my dad run the business, which freed me up and gave me time to decide what I wanted to do. I knew I could always gill net with any one of my uncles and cousins. Back in those days, I think fishermen were getting about a nickel a pound for mullet. Another option was to build myself some crab baskets, fix up my dad's old boat, and start crabbing for a living. As long as I didn't have to cook or clean crabs, I could handle them. If all went well, I could save up my money and build myself a little bay shrimper.

As a last resort, I figured I could take up oystering; even though, I had never been fond of that job. Standing up in a boat and clanging together heavy tongs to harvest oysters from the bottom of the bay just didn't appeal to me. That was backbreaking work, and I really didn't want any part of it.

Since I had always enjoyed carpentry work, when I wasn't fishing, I figured I could help out with building the new house. My two older sisters had already left home, but there were still six of us crammed into the little house next door to where my family was planning to build a larger home. The sooner we got the new house built, the better.

I also thought about attending college with the new GI Bill. I already knew a real cute girl who attended FSCW in Tallahassee who had promised to show me around. With the enactment of the GI Bill, men were now allowed to attend the previously all women institution. I even thought that I might major in History. I had always enjoyed history and still do today.

Regardless, for the moment, I was headed home to become a fisherman like so many generations before me. Living and working on the water was part of my heritage; it was all I had ever known for the first 18 years of my life. I had watched, with pride, as my father worked hard to provide for his family. Fishing was an honorable profession, and I felt very blessed to be able to return home and start a new life making a living off the water.

I began to think about all of those who were left behind, young men who would never return home to start a new life. I thought about the potential that lay buried in graves so far away; young men, in the prime of life, young men who would have become doctors, lawyers, professors or maybe even President. I decided, that somehow, I had to honor them; and the only way I could think of to do that was to get on with my life - get on with my life because I could.

On that final bus ride home, I was suddenly overwhelmed by a sense of hope. I wasn't worried about my future. I knew that I was going to be okay. For whatever reason, I had faced and survived 35 combat missions against Nazi Germany. Surely, I could bravely face and survive whatever lay ahead for me as I started my new life.

Epilogue

After the war, I did return home and work in the family seafood business for a couple of years. To everyone's relief, during that time, we did finish the new house. Times were still tough economically, so I decided to go back into the Service. I re-enlisted over at Tyndall Army-Air Field in Panama City and was very fortunate to be stationed there in crash rescue with the fire department.

While in Panama City, I met my wife of over 60 years, Virginia Scott, from Abbeville, Alabama. We have two daughters, Wanda and Barbara, and one grandson, Brandon Goodwin. Ginny and I are very fortunate to have all our family living nearby.

I remained in the Air Force until 1967 when I retired as a Master Sergeant. Most of my military career was spent in aircraft-weapons maintenance systems. After retiring, I worked with the Post Office in Tampa, Florida; Firestone Tire and Rubber Co. in Albany, Georgia; and with my brother's construction business on St. George Island, Florida.

For the past 20 years or so, Ginny and I have lived in Lynn Haven, Florida. Over the years, we have both enjoyed restoring and buying and selling antiques. In our younger days, we both played golf. I have a wood-working shop and continue to enjoy tinkering. One of my favorite past-time activities is working crossword puzzles, an activity I've enjoyed as long as I can remember. I still enjoy listening to beautiful music. Both my wife and I are avid gardeners and still maintain a beautiful yard as well as a small vegetable garden. Our house has a wonderful view of North Bay - that's a good thing because I just can't seem to breathe if I can't see the water.

Cold Biscuits

by Billy Samford

Cold biscuits, cold mullet, cold beans for my fair, I'll cast
my net into the sea just to feed my family dear

Cold biscuits, cold mullet, cold beans for my fair, I'll take
this food with a grateful thanks to the Lord I love so dear

Blessed with a land of plenty,
Blessed for the bountiful sea,
Blessed for my wife and children, and the life they share
with me

Cold biscuits, cold mullet, cold beans for my fair, I'll cast
my net into the sea just to feed my family dear

I'll cast my net in the morning,
I'll cast my net at night
I'll tong the beds for my family dear
Just to make a better life

Cold biscuits, cold mullet, cold beans for my fair, I'll cast
my net into the sea just to feed my family dear

No job, no money
Not a penny to my name
My family ain't never missed a meal
And their clothes are warm and clean

Cold biscuits, cold mullet, cold beans for my fair, I'll cast
my net into the sea just to feed my family dear

Cold biscuits, cold mullet, cold beans for my fair, I'll cast
my net into the sea just to feed my family dear

I'll take this food with grateful thanks
To the Lord I love so dear........

To order more copies of Last Roll Call, or to contact the author, please visit:

Ken Tucker at
kenstucker@aol.com

and

Wanda Tucker Goodwin at
wtgoodwin@aol.com